A PRIMER IN
PASTORAL CARE

CREATIVE PASTORAL CARE AND COUNSELING SERIES

A PRIMER IN PASTORAL CARE

JEANNE STEVENSON-MOESSNER

FORTRESS PRESS   MINNEAPOLIS

A PRIMER IN PASTORAL CARE
Creative Pastoral Care and Counseling Series

Scripture quotations are from the New Revised Standard Version Bible, copyright © 1989 by the Division of Christian Education of the National Council of the Churches of Christ in the USA and used by permission.
Cover image: © Comstock Images, comstock.com.
Author photo: © Weber Portrait Design.

Library of Congress Cataloging-in-Publication Data

Moessner, Jeanne Stevenson, 1948–
  A primer in pastoral care / Jeanne Stevenson-Moessner.
    p. cm. — (Creative pastoral care and counseling series)
  Includes bibliographical references.
  ISBN 0-8006-3760-7 (alk. paper)
  1. Pastoral care. 2. Pastoral counseling. 3. Pastoral theology.
  I. Title. II. Series.
  BV4011.3.M64 2005
  253—dc22
                                                         2005015688

The paper used in this publication meets the minimum requirements of American National Standard for Information Sciences — Permanence of Paper for Printed Library Materials, ANSI Z329.48-1984.

Manufactured in the U.S.A.

09   08   07   06   05   1   2   3   4   5   6   7   8   9   10

*To my students
at the University of Dubuque Theological Seminary
who may be ten minutes from a cornfield but
who are surely in the heartland of God*

CONTENTS

EDITOR'S FOREWORD

I am sure that most readers have had the experience of browsing through the bookstore at the annual church convention or pastoral conference when, there on the table, is a book that you recognize as something you should have read when you first entered ministry. It is such a simple yet profound book addressing something that you have been dealing with ever since seminary. Well, that was my response when I first read a draft of *A Primer in Pastoral Care*. Jeanne Stevenson-Moessner has fashioned a basic pastoral care text to assist in the emotional and spiritual education of pastoral caregivers. It is a simple, clear-cut introduction to the what, why, and how of pastoral care for beginning pastors, seminarians, and Clinical Pastoral Education students, lay leaders, and lay pastors.

Jeanne Stevenson-Moessner is Associate Professor of Pastoral Theology and Christian Formation at the University of Dubuque Theological Seminary, in Dubuque, Iowa, as well as an ordained minister in the Presbyterian Church (U.S.A.). *A Primer in Pastoral Care* reflects her own experience in offering pastoral care and twenty years of teaching the subject in a seminary.

Stevenson-Moessner presents her image of pastoral care as the interplay of love of God, love of neighbor, and love of self. *A Primer in Pastoral Care* is meant to engender "confidence and caring" in the initiate, and to assuage the fear and anxiety that naturally occur when accompanying people in their journeys through the "valley of the shadow," through their trials and suffering. Through skilled use of the parables of the Good Samaritan and the Good Shepherd, along with stories from her own experience, Stevenson-Moessner imparts genuine wisdom and meaningful support to those who courageously dare to offer pastoral caregiving ministry in whatever situation.

A Primer in Pastoral Care, in a mere seven chapters, gives the reader a base from which to offer pastoral care. The book is a "primer"—not a comprehensive text, but a good beginning. Indeed, it is a useful refresher course that reminds seasoned caregivers what is the basis of the care they offer. Chapter 1, "The

One-Room Schoolhouse," talks about the first day of class—the first times we try to care for others and what can be expected. The second chapter, "The Grammar of Care," addresses the desire that most of us have to "fix things." With the acronym "grammar," Stevenson-Moessner suggests how we position ourselves in relation to those we care for. Chapter 3, "The Prism of Pastoral Care," uses several images of pastoral care from scripture to suggest different models of pastoral caregiving and helps the reader to choose one.

Chapter 4, "The Community as Classroom: Avoiding Compassion Fatigue," covers how caregivers need to attend to their own spiritual and emotional well-being. Burnout occurs when caregivers do not care for themselves as well as their charges. Chapters 5 and 6, "The Open Classroom: Places of Care" and "More Places of Care," and chapter 7, "An Alphabet of Grace," cover some of the more common pastoral care situations we encounter. Stevenson-Moessner provides readers with ways they can help people who are ill, in the hospital, dying, depressed, or bereaved, or in other types of situations that are common to the pastoral care enterprise.

I am confident that reading *A Primer in Pastoral Care* will strengthen and enrich your pastoral care, counseling, and general ministry. Stevenson-Moessner brings to her work the wisdom of over twenty years of experience as a pastor, counselor, and seminary professor. The scope and quality of the care you offer to others are certain to benefit from her knowledge and sound guidance.

Howard W. Stone

ACKNOWLEDGMENTS

A sabbatical semester granted to me by the University of Dubuque provided a break in time and space for me to write this primer. Throughout the quietly altered rhythm of my academic life, Howard Stone remained a constant, insightful, and faithful editor. At Fortress Press, he was joined by Michael West, Abby Coles, and James Korsmo. It has been an invigorating team.

My days were spent surrounded by 450 dedicated, passionate Franciscan nuns at Shalom Retreat Center, near Mount St. Francis, on the outskirts of Dubuque. I am convinced that I could not have written this book in the way I did without their encouraging environment. In particular, I was greeted each day by Sister Margaret Jungers and Connie Wilgenbusch and was also encouraged by the presence of Sister Michelle Nemmers and Sister Dolores Ullrich. I am glad I found the gift store and the "sweet shop," but I shall miss the smiles, the calm, and the sense that I was a sister too.

My evenings were spent with my husband, Dave, and our two children, David and Jean, at our home in Dubuque. My husband's devotion to biblical studies and my teenagers' *joie de vivre* kept me stimulated, challenged, and engaged with the world in a way that was as holy as my temporary hermitage. Our household is blessed by the presence of Linda Wlochal, who nourishes us with her cooking, jokes, and stories.

A number of students at the University of Dubuque will peer out from these pages. John Gay, ministerial student and work-study student, has carefully worked all semester to tidy my manuscript and to solidify endnotes. I appreciate his thorough dedication to usher this little book into the hands of readers.

I acknowledge all that my students have taught me, here at Dubuque for eight years, earlier at Columbia Theological Seminary (Atlanta) for thirteen years, at Candler School of Theology (Atlanta) and at Samford University (Birmingham) in my capacity as adjunct, at the Black Forest Academy (Kandern, Germany), and in my first position at St. Mary's Episcopal School (Memphis). Students never come as a blank slate. This primer is proof of that.

Throughout this year, some extraordinary colleagues and friends called regularly to check on me, including Dr. Martha Robbins, Dr. Nan Hawkes, Rev. Dr. Susan Sharpe, Rev. Dr. Joan Murray, Dr. Mary Lynn Dell, Jane Lange, and Dr. Elizabeth Liebert. During the 2003–2004 academic year, I deeply appreciated the support of Dr. Shannon Jung, Dr. Lyle Vander Broek, Dr. Elmer Colyer, and Dr. Phil Jamieson. It is also a source of joy to have Dr. Elizabeth Platt across the hallway at the seminary and Dr. Bonnie Sue Lewis next door. Rev. Dr. Teresa Snorton, executive director of the Association for Clinical Pastoral Education, and I labored together on the steering committee of the Society for Pastoral Theology even during my sabbatical. Her remarkable efficiency as an administrator made this possible.

Today, my sabbatical is over, and I go to clean out my room at Shalom Retreat Center. My room was a holy space for the writing of this primer. Since a primer was originally a prayer book, let it be my prayer that in the reading of these pages, you will find some holy spaces too.

INTRODUCTION

I was nudged into a situation that a qualified and skillfully trained chaplain would enter with awe and healthy fear.

My great-grandmother was a teacher in a one-room schoolhouse in Mississippi in the 1800s. She probably used a "primer," an introductory text, to appeal simultaneously to a variety of ages and stages of experience in her classroom. With the use of a primer, not only were differing levels taught but the older students could mentor younger students in the fundamentals of learning. In *A Primer in Pastoral Care*, I shall strive to create such a "learning community" within the readership so that those of you with more pastoral exposure can help those of you who are beginners when this text is used in a group setting. This "learning community" will be inclusive of all diversities.

My great-grandmother was also an artist. She has left behind some vibrant oil paintings, three of which hang in my home. Following her artistic method, I will not proceed in 1-2-3 fashion, like a paint-by-number kit. Rather, I will depict a still life of situations of care, with vistas opening to the varieties of pastoral response and glimpses of a larger landscape in ministry.

This book began with an urgent e-mail from Chaplain Judy Mulock, a pastor in Iowa:

> Could I ask for your professional help in suggesting two books or resources for a 2-day lay pastors' course I'm to teach in 2005? I'm a chaplain in Waterloo . . . and I'm 20 years out of seminary, but I want to provide the most up-to-date, well-balanced and practical materials for these lay pastors in the area of pastoral care.

The Iowa pastor needed a written introduction to pastoral care, more basic than the well-constructed foundational text that I have used for years at seminary level. She sought something that could be adapted to a weekend or two-day training retreat for lay persons. Could I help? This request and similar queries that followed it have led to the creation of this primer.

My students at the University of Dubuque Theological Seminary become a community of learners each spring in a required course, Introduction to Pastoral Care. Through their verbal etchings and snapshot stories that appear in this text, they will invite you into their open classroom. Although some seminary students enter the classroom believing they know nothing about pastoral care, they soon learn they are not a tabula rasa or blank slate. They all come with memories of effective or ineffective care that they have received. You come with recollections as well. Thus, I would encourage you to start with this question: What is your most meaningful memory of receiving effective pastoral care? Your answer to this question will probably form the cornerstone in your foundation of offering effective care to others.

As you consider this first assignment of remembering, let me summarize. This book is an attempt to support you in your courageous caregiving, whether as a lay commissioned pastor, lay member of a congregation, seminarian, clinical pastoral education intern, or newly installed pastor. It contains some of the wisdom I have acquired in the thirty years since I had the following agonizing encounter as a college student.

I had come to the intensive care unit of Vanderbilt Hospital to see my college roommate, who had been rushed there for emergency surgery. After calling her parents who lived across the country, I had hurried to the hospital so that she would have a friend. Perhaps I had mentioned to the nurse that I was chaplain of a sorority. It remains unclear to me even now why the nurse asked me to help in the waiting room.

A family unknown to me was sitting helplessly, overcome with shock and numbness. The wife and children had been given the medical verdict: their husband/father had just died of head trauma following a car accident. His body lay in a bed in the intensive care unit, a bed separated from my roommate by a white linen curtain. Now I, a college student and "chaplain" of my social club, was expected to help. I was nudged into a situation that a qualified and skillfully trained chaplain would enter with awe and healthy fear.

This primer contains some of the insight and knowledge that I have acquired since I was thrust into that hospital chamber of pain and death. I will draw from the experience of many others who have offered pastoral care, whether in the antechambers of joys or in the archives of grief, whether in the celebrations of life or the ceremonies of loss. Confidence will come with the wisdom in these pages as you continue to work with compassion alongside the one who is called the Great Physician. You will never be alone in your caring. As you read further, you will become more aware of various types of teamwork in caregiving. As you colabor with Christ and with helping professionals in ministry, you will enter holy spaces never before imagined. Taking care of yourself will be as important as taking care of another as you venture forth. Let us begin.

• **Question**

What is *your* most meaningful memory of receiving pastoral care?

Chapter One

THE ONE-ROOM SCHOOLHOUSE

I think the greatest gift she brought was her presence. She did not worry about saying the right thing to ease all our troubles; she simply shared in our troubles with us.

Pastoral care has many faces and takes many forms. In short, pastoral care is an outreach of compassion often accompanied by an action of care. That action can be as ordinary as offering food to someone who is isolated and lonely or as complicated as intervening in a medical crisis. Let me illustrate.

A seminary student training to be a minister was asked the same question that you considered in the introduction: What is your most meaningful memory of receiving pastoral care? This student was tackling this question as a homework assignment. He thought and thought. He first wrote about his parents' divorce and the way the church reached out to his parents. A group of men volunteered to reroof his family's house because finances were limited. That action was pastoral care. His brother ended up in the hospital, and care was extended to the brother through hospital visits. That was pastoral care. Now you may be thinking, I cannot roof a house and I hate hospitals. Read on.

As one seminarian wrote: "I've never been very sick or broken a bone. No pastor ever visited my hospital bed, or came to visit my house. I never received counseling at the church. I've never received food or money in response to some need I expressed at the church."[1] All of the actions this student describes here, with the exception of the counseling, would be considered pastoral care. Counseling is a separate category, one that usually entails three to five visits and is most often conducted by someone trained in listening skills and counseling techniques. The seminarian had received none of the above. What he did receive that was so transformative was strikingly "simple": a box of cookies. He continues:

The only thing I remember being directly for me was the box of cookies that the ladies of the church sent me while I was at school. Sure they sent them to everyone, but they remembered me, and they didn't have to. I appreciated it, and the cookies were good. It felt good to know I was remembered. It wasn't incredibly meaningful, but it was an act of kindness in Christ's name. I hadn't told them I was lonely, and actually I wasn't lonely. I was quite happy being away from home, but they meant well, and knowing they remembered me made me lonely to be with them again, I guess. That means it was in response to a need.[2]

You may at times be asked to offer pastoral care in an unfamiliar setting. You may also opt to receive additional training so that you feel comfortable in these challenging settings. However, most often God will seek to match you with your given abilities. Remember: if you can't do carpentry, there are always the cookies!

LEVELS OF LEARNING, LEVELS OF CARE

In the one-room schoolhouse first discussed in the introduction, there were almost as many levels of learning as there were students. In the same way, there are many different levels of care, from mailing cookies to responding to cardiac arrest. Following is an example at one extreme end of the spectrum in terms of pastoral care situations.

Tom was looking somewhat blanched as he sat on the front row in my Foundations of Pastoral Care class. Tom had missed a few days of class due to health-related problems, which he thought was the flu. During the class break on this particular Tuesday, after admitting he had not taken time to eat lunch, he accepted a couple of cookies from a classmate. A few minutes before the class period was to end, Tom rose quietly, staggered down the aisle between desks, exited the classroom, and collapsed on a couch in the hallway. A student trained in CPR and I followed him out immediately. Tom was having difficulty breathing and thought it was his heart.

This cardiac emergency required instant pastoral teamwork with the following team players. I functioned as organizer. A student with a cell phone handy was the messenger to 911. The CPR-trained student knelt at the foot of the couch. A former nurse, now

in seminary as a second career, passed by, and we grabbed him to
assist. Four students became hall monitors, clearing the hallways
and keeping other students from clogging the avenues through
which a hospital emergency team would soon pass. Not knowing
which entrance the ambulance would choose, three more students
were stationed as scouts at each entrance to the building. They
were to stand outside and wave the emergency medical personnel
into the correct corridors. The majority of the students were asked
to remain in the classroom and pray. Although they may have felt
ineffective, these members of the team had a responsibility as serious as any other. All in all, this team effort involved almost seventy
people. I acted as liaison to the student's family, who lived three
hours away, calling on a cell phone as we all awaited the ambulance. All seventy of us who participated in this rescue effort never
lost one minute to confusion or delay. It was as if God had orches-
trated a precise support team for this collapsed student. He survived to tell his story.

In class, we had been reading Howard Stone's *Crisis Counseling*
and reciting the ABCs on pastoral care in crisis settings: **A**chieve
contact, **B**oil down the problem to its essentials, and **C**ope actively
with the problem.[3] None of us pretended to be the physician on
call or the ambulance personnel. We responded with great speed,
with an unearthly calm, with actions, and with prayer. The students
acknowledged my training by allowing me to be the coordinator,
and I, in turn, called forth individuals according to their gifts.

Both instances of pastoral care discussed here, from boxing
cookies to responding to a medical emergency, required teamwork.
The women of the church baking cookies for the college students
is an excellent example of *pastoral initiative*. The women did not
wait for a college student to be lonely. Instead, they reached out
to make a connection. In the case of the medical crisis, *pastoral
intervention* was the response to a life-threatening situation. You
can tell from these two dissimilar examples what a wide spectrum
is involved when we consider giving pastoral care. There are different levels of care just as there were different levels of learning in
the one-room schoolhouse.

To put this another way, a spectrum of offerings exists in
pastoral care, from sending cookies to helping in a cardiac emergency. Most often, acts of pastoral care are simple ones. People in

transition, loss, or disappointment as well as those in joyous occasions can need help with basic tasks. Bringing a meal, cutting the grass, or running an errand not only is a supportive gesture but also represents Christ to these people. As you push the garbage cans out to the street, you can prayerfully say, "These hands are doing Christ's work" and "These feet are Christ's feet." When you intentionally perform an act of compassion in Christ's name, you are standing in for Christ; you are representing Christ to those in need. Very basic tasks are transformed into holy actions when you colabor with Christ. Imagine Christ at your side as you deliver a hot meal to the family of a newborn. Talk to Christ as you grocery shop for a parishioner recovering from surgery. These are devotional moments because they further a developing relationship with the one in whose name you serve. The term "pastoral" derives from the Greek word for "shepherd." You are following the Good Shepherd as you serve and represent him with your voice, arms, and legs. This is pastoral care in its truest sense.

MENTORING AND DISCIPLESHIP

In the one-room schoolhouse, the teacher would try to address all students at their various learning stages. At times, an older and wiser student was used to mentor or coach a younger or less-schooled student. In this way, the more advanced students served an unofficial apprenticeship. Perhaps they were the predecessors of student teachers.

In a comparable way, members of a congregation can be mentored or trained in pastoral care. This alleviates some of the demands of the ordained pastor, priest, or minister. It also activates the reality of the "priesthood of believers," which is a focus of the book of Hebrews. When a layperson is trained in the task of caring, this is a valid form of discipleship. Consider the following example, in which the members of one church in western North Dakota had to assume the role of pastoral outreach.

Eighteen months into his ministry in this small rural community, Pastor Arley slipped on a steep concrete incline during a major snowstorm and sustained a spinal cord and head injury. He hovered between life and death for nineteen days in the intensive care unit of the nearest hospital. He survived, but his speech, motor, and bodily functions were compromised and he was no longer able to minister. To qualify for disability, he and his family would have to move from the parsonage and Pastor Arley would have to surrender this appointment in the United Methodist Church. He was looking at loss of a full-time income, mounting medical bills, and a rising depression. His wife, Peggy, was in charge of the household and the upbringing of the children.

The parish needed a minister, and the minister needed a home and an income. At this point, Peggy stepped forward. She agreed to assume the duties of a full-time lay minister in exchange for three things: assistance in taking Arley to therapy three times a week (a two-hour round trip), childcare for her children, and most important, participation in ministry *by the members of the congregation themselves.* Now the laity had to assume such responsibilities as general visitation.

A metamorphosis occurred. This sleepy, fractured congregation began to gain strength and healing. Their transformation paralleled Arley's progress and recovery.

As Peggy Ellingson writes: "[The church] began to heal right along with Arley. As Arley reached a milestone in recovery, so did the church. They seemed to come alive, with a renewed sense of hope, because they had been empowered to do ministry themselves. They began to regain some of the spirit of community they had lost and started to reach out to one another."[4]

This is an extreme example of the functional priesthood of believers. However, it points to the potential for lay members of a congregation to be transformed into "lay ministers." By the way, Peggy eventually ended up going to seminary. Her call, which had been dormant, was activated by the sudden crisis of need.

THE FIRST DAY OF SCHOOL

Whether in the one-room schoolhouse or at the major university, there is something about the first day of school that is exciting and sometimes frightening. One wonders: Who will the teacher(s) be? Will I rise to the challenge of the new material? Will I feel inadequate to the task(s)? Am I too old to learn?

Even seasoned teachers have some healthy anxiety on the first day of school. They ask themselves the following: Are the lesson plans adequate? Am I thoroughly prepared? Do I know enough to teach *these* students? Will there be challenges, such as disciplinary problems?

If you have some anxiety or fear about learning to be a pastoral caregiver, that feeling is normal. Pastoral care in the church can engage us in chapters of life that are unfamiliar, uncomfortable, or painful. An excellent first step is to name and then claim your fear, anxiety, or nervousness. You may also want to claim the anticipation, the joy, and the excitement of venturing forth with Christ into places of need. There are four basic emotions or feelings: mad, sad, glad, and afraid. Take a moment for personal inventory. Which are you feeling? Perhaps a combination of two or three?

When I was a teenager, I danced in a ballet company. For four years, each time the music would begin and the outer curtain would ascend, I had a terrible case of "butterflies" in my stomach, or nervousness. Although it got better, it never went away completely, even after opening night. After three years of this, I asked a ballet master how to deal with this onset of jitters. He said: "If you didn't get 'butterflies' when the music starts, you would be a ham [show-off]." I was so relieved to know I was in the range of "normalcy" that I claimed my feeling of fear, accepted it, and danced with all my heart.

Ministry is like that. Claim your nervousness and offer it to God. It is normal to feel anxious in ministry, especially when we stand at the portal of a hospital room or at the entrance to a waiting room or place of visitation. It may help to visualize Christ standing beside you, holding your hand, guiding you, preceding you. You will never be alone. Ironically, the times I have felt the most inadequate often become the occasions when Christ's presence is made more manifest. I believe I have to trust more and allow the Holy Spirit to prompt me. This never fails because the one who is our mentor is trustworthy.

I once heard the story of a man who nervously entered the funeral parlor where a dear friend lay in his coffin. The friend's wife was receiving visitors as she stood by the open coffin. This nervous man felt so inadequate that he didn't know what to say. When he reached the widow, he clasped her hand warmly in his, looked at her lovingly with tears in his eyes, and said, "Congratulations." What is amazing is that the widow never noticed the wrong word. She was too intent on his loving face, his genuine gesture, his kindness, his grief. You see, Christ was there, embracing the two well-meaning people, and Christ's presence was more than adequate to compensate for the man's slip of the tongue.[5]

CLASSROOM ETIQUETTE

Most teachers establish ground rules or classroom etiquette fairly early in the school year, perhaps even on the first day. In a similar way, established guides exist for caring conduct. Tolerance and respect for "the other" are foremost, especially in crises and loss. We allow the person to whom we are ministering to take the lead in regard to what he or she needs. It is not our place as caregiver to negate or deny the person's feelings. Rather, it is our role to validate those feelings and to create a safe place where they can be expressed in the person's own timing. Thus much of our role is to listen, to attend, to wait patiently, to accompany, to be there as a presence—a pastoral presence—representing the church and Jesus Christ.

One seminarian recounts her most meaningful experience of receiving effective care. It was in the hospital following her cesarian delivery, the birth of an unhealthy son with medical complications. She described it as "a very uncomfortable unknowing situation" with sketchy details of prognosis and treatment. She couldn't nurse or hold her son, and she was still healing from her surgery. Then her pastor walked in. The woman writes:

> She [the pastor] followed our lead, talking small talk when we did and worried talk when we did. She never made the claim that all would be fine, but instead reminded us that no matter what, we would have support from God (and of course, the [Methodist] conference). She asked if we would like prayer, which we did, and visited a bit more before she left. No fireworks went off, and in fact there were even awkward moments. But in a way, sharing *in the awkwardness* was sharing in our uncertainty, and sharing in the silence was sharing in our unknowing. I think the greatest gift she brought was her presence. . . . She did not worry about saying the right thing to ease all our troubles; she simply shared in our troubles with us.[6]

// This is incarnational presence, the willingness to share in someone's situation, in the person's discomfort and awkwardness, if need be. This is what Christ did in the incarnation; he shared in our lot and dwelt among humankind. //

// In pastoral care, we accept what people say and feel, no matter how outlandish it may sound to us. In the rare instances that people express suicidal or homicidal thoughts or expose sexual abuse, we do need to respond in a certain way, which will be discussed later. We also need to honor the questions that surface in times of loss and transition. In the days of the one-room schoolhouse, a student considered stupid or foolish would be isolated, made to sit on a stool in the corner and wear a dunce's cap. In pastoral care, there is no dunce's corner for "stupid" questions. We never humiliate or shame; rather, we respect the other person and his or her emotions. //

In summary, we honor the other person and accompany that person in his or her need. Perhaps you remember a time of loneliness in a school setting, maybe after a move or a change of schools or after an unsuccessful attempt to join a club or society. If so, you may have been fortunate to have a classroom teacher, a guidance counselor, a homeroom teacher, an older student, a coach, a friend, a pastor, or a chaplain help you during your transition or loneliness. Christian companionship with compassion is what we offer to others in pastoral care as we, the caregivers, remain faithful to Christ as companion.

• Question
In the teamwork of pastoral care, how are *you* uniquely gifted as a team player? (If you are in a group, you may want to solicit input from others in the group who know you.)

Chapter Two

THE GRAMMAR OF CARE: POINTERS AND PRECEPTS

In school, we memorized the alphabet, our ABCs. However, the grammar of care is not like that. It is not reciting. It is listening to others' words, hearing between the words, and being open to both a spoken text and an unspoken text. It involves reading between the lines.

It is a natural tendency to want to "fix things" when someone is in need of our care. This seems especially true if you are a person of compassion, an individual who is responsible and conscientious, a firstborn child, or the sibling who was designated as caregiver in the family system. More often than not, we are invited to listen to a person's sometimes painful or unhappy story. Sometimes, as we create a safe environment for a person, we actually "hear them into speech."[1] This newfound expression comes after trust has been established, after the person feels that he or she can speak without being embarrassed or belittled, and after the person knows that what he or she has to offer will be valued. Trust and safety issues are crucial in pastoral care, particularly for those who are in minority or devalued positions in our society because of socioeconomic, gender, racial ethnic, political, or cultural factors. Persons who are mentally and physically challenged also look for places of trust and safety.

Occasionally, if we enter the caring relationship as a holy space, if we are centered spiritually, we might even hear the silence before the speaking.[2] One student communicated this profound truth through a poem:

Too Deep for Words
My soul's assailed
with hurts—
Too deep for words

There's no way to let them out,
Trapped down in depths too deep to be known,
Except in darkest night or when chance encounter
With kindred life cracks wide the unfathomed orb.
Kept there for fear that letting loose will
Cause pain deeper still.
Thank God for times
when hurts—
Too deep for words,
Can speak through Spirit Holy
who moans and groans
With sighs—
Too deep for words.[3]

It is the Spirit Holy who prompts us to hear the silence too deep for words. Again, we are expected neither to fix anything nor to do something. We are the "kindred life" that becomes available through "chance" encounter, which we call a pastoral encounter. Trusting in God's guidance, we realize that the encounter is not by chance but by design.

Pastoral caregivers have sometimes entered a room where the hurt was too deep for words, as in the following example. One student pastor sat quietly in the corner of a hospital room while the agonized family came to terms with the sudden death of a loved one. There was wailing and moaning and cursing as well as the dazed silence of some family members. All of these forms of shock and anger are appropriate, of course, in the presence of death. And so the student pastor sat there quietly and felt "the assaults" being made on the souls of those gathered around the deathbed. The hurts were too deep for words. He sat patiently; he prayed quietly and did not flinch with the outcries. In due time, he left without having said one single word. The next day, as funeral preparations were under way, the family member most directly affected by the death approached the student pastor. What she said amazed him. "Pastor," she said with great feeling., "Thank you for all you did for us yesterday in that hospital room. I couldn't have made it without you." He hadn't uttered one word! Their pain was too deep for words. In many cases, the "grammar" of pastoral care, ironically, may involve silence.

Here is a way to understand the grammar of pastoral care. It is not necessary to memorize the following list, but all of the items are important to include in your caregiving.

> G: Get into a receptive posture.
> R: Receive whatever the other person offers.
> A: Acknowledge the other person's feelings.
> M: Make a holy, welcoming, and boundaried space.
> M: Match the other person's needs with your caregiving.
> A: Accept the other person as he or she is.
> R: Reach out.

This last step—reaching out—may entail some form of guidance. However, no judgment, teaching, or preaching is involved, although there may be modeling. Reaching out may involve an action or a sacrament, such as offering Holy Communion or the Eucharist. It could also involve finding other helping professionals to help you give more holistic care to the hurting individual. Enlisting specialists to help you provide a support network is always a sign of strength, not of weakness.

These elements of the grammar of care will be illustrated in the following case study. In a way, this is a worst-case scenario because of the isolated location and the paucity of referral sources involved. However, if we go through this scenario together, you will gain confidence for other situations that are less challenging.

"THE GREAT SAVOONGA COUNSELOR"

Savoonga, Alaska, is a very remote village on an island about twenty-two miles from the coast of Siberia. The Savoonga Presbyterian Church is the only active church on the island. There are no community mental health centers or counselors on the island, only one physician's assistant. The following story was told by the student intern who served as pastor of the Presbyterian Church.[4]

As the student pastor's family was heading upstairs for bed, there came a knock at the door. A local young man asked to come in and talk. This young man was the relative of an active session member who had referred him to the student pastor. Let us walk through the grammar of pastoral care as it unfolded.

G: Get into a Receptive Posture

This is difficult when you have had a long day and are heading up the stairs to bed. At the sound of the knock, the student intern told his wife and young son to go on to bed. He opened the door, and there stood a young villager who wanted to come in and talk. I can well imagine that this young intern was tired. His body was unwinding for bedtime. This intern had also been trained at seminary to pace himself and to take care of himself. This self-care is an essential for continuing in caregiving. You take care of yourself; you love yourself just as you love others. We can hope that because this student intern had been eating well, getting regular sleep, exercising, and making leisure time, he was able to summon a reserve of energy for this unexpected nocturnal visit. Remember, at this point, that our student intern did not know the reason for the visit. Perhaps the student intern engaged in self-talk, such as admitting to himself that he was tired but resolving that he would call on the Holy Spirit for an extra measure of life-giving energy in this late hour.

R: Receive What the Other Person Offers

After telling the visitor that he was glad he had come, the student intern listened to what clinicians call the "presenting problem." This is the expressed or spoken "reason" for seeking out a pastor or counselor. Often, there is more to the situation than what is presented. However, in this particular case, this nocturnal visitor got right to the core reason. The visitor said that he didn't want to live any longer and that that night would be his last.

This is one of the most startling and frightening utterances you can receive, no matter how seasoned you become. A statement like this must be taken very seriously. The student intern did not fall off his seat, he did not jump up in shock, and he did not try to dismiss the confession. He received it calmly and genuinely.

Feeling that he was being taken seriously, the visitor began to tell his life's story, which involved the murder of his mother and father, other family tragedies, a history of drug abuse and depression, feelings of guilt, his state of poverty, and the discrimination he had felt because he had dark skin. How, he asked, could a loving God allow this much tragedy to happen to just one person, to him?

A: Acknowledge the Other Person's Feelings

The student pastor acknowledged the man's feelings by admitting that he had also had times of doubt and depression himself. Here, you must be careful to keep this admission short and brief. You do not want to unload your own burdens when a vulnerable person comes to you for support. The student pastor simply made a move to give credibility to this outpouring of "irreligious" feelings. The pastor sought to acknowledge and connect; he wanted to put the night visitor at ease.

M: Make a Holy, Welcoming, and Boundaried Space

The student pastor's living room was welcoming. He had put a pot of coffee on early in the conversation. Sometimes, drinking something hot or cold helps to "ground a person" to reality. You can prompt the person to feel the liquid slide down the throat and remind the person to stay connected body and soul. The student pastor offered a welcoming space by his relaxed body language, which said: "I have time for you. You must not hurry through your story. I am not shocked or revolted by what you say. I am with you."

The student pastor kept his own comments brief. He told the man that he had also experienced "inconsistencies" in the nature of the omniscient, omnipotent, and loving God. He was careful to boundary or contain his stories, because he did not want to overload the hurting visitor.

M: Match the Other Person's Needs with Your Caregiving

The visitor was in pain, and the conversation went on for several hours. The recurring question was as follows: "If we were really the children of a loving God, then how could that loving God still allow suffering and abuse?" The pastor did his best to answer this most difficult question, which theologians term the theodicy question.

At a point of verbal impasse, the pastor's five-year-old son, Ian, came slowly down the stairs, rubbing his sleepy eyes, wearing only his underwear, and revealing a completely innocent demeanor. He said, "I have to go pee." With that statement, both the pastor and the visitor had to smile and shared the common bond of being fathers of completely innocent children. At this crucial point in the pastoral caregiving, the student pastor used the family situation as a point of connection. He said: "Watch what Ian does when he comes out of the bathroom."

The doorknob turned, and Ian ran straight over to the arms of his father. He crawled onto his lap and hugged him like it was the last time he would see him. With kisses and a bear hug, Ian said "good-night" to both men and climbed carefully back to the second floor of the manse. The pastor used what had occurred to ask: "What would happen if my son Ian had fallen down those stairs and died? Would that make my love for him any less?"

The night visitor started crying and sobbing for many years' worth of pain. He finally said, "I get it." Evidently, nothing the student pastor had said the entire evening had made any sense to him, yet a chubby five-year-old boy had brought him back to the basic understanding of who God is: love. It was an incarnational lesson, one translated into flesh, and it brought an insight that the student pastor's theological ramblings had not done. The Holy Spirit had used the pastor's familial context and his over-flowing love for his son to illustrate the love of God as Father. In this way, the visitor's need was matched with what the student pastor had to give.

A: Accept the Other Person as He or She Is

The night visitor had experienced discrimination because of his skin color. Although his mother was Siberian Yupik, his father was non-native, and he was darker in skin. For this reason, his wife's family had ostracized him.

As pastoral caregivers, we will need to examine our preju-dices and move into a place of openness to differences. We will be asked to suspend judgment and to withhold our preferences. We can do this as we imagine ourselves at the foot of the cross of Christ with those from whom we differ—for Christ died for them too.

R: Reach Out

In writing up this case, the student pastor decided that his five-year-old was "The Great Savoonga Counselor," in cooperation with the Holy Spirit, of course. If the situation had not moved along as it did, the student pastor would have had to take other measures to help. An assessment of the man's suicide risk would have been taken; the visitor would not have been left alone, and the help of the physician's assistant could have been summoned. At daybreak, transport of the suicidal person to a neighboring island could have been arranged. For a person who is genuinely suicidal, a network of professionals is warranted. We take all threats of suicide seriously, especially if the person has already made a plan to carry out the suicide.[5]

THE SUBTEXT

In pastoral care, we listen for the subtext. We assume there is more going on than is being said, so we stay attuned for the subplot, for the things that are too painful to be named or spoken. Emotional communication or emotional grammar is always going on alongside the verbal. The Holy Spirit comes to our aid if we are open to this type of intervention.

In school, we memorize the alphabet, our ABCs. However, the grammar of care is not like that. It is not reciting. It is listening to others' words, hearing between the words, and being open to both a spoken text and an unspoken subtext. It involves reading between the lines.

You have perhaps attended a meeting with a sense of something else going on in addition to the stated agenda. This might be a power play, unspoken expectations, manipulation, or other issues that have not been expressed. There is a separate agenda going on "under the table" or in the "back boardroom."

Perhaps you have been to a social event where you sense other feelings, intentions, interactions, or posturing going on beneath the surface chitchat and social niceties. For example, if people are too solicitous and too complimentary, you wonder what else is going on with them. Do they want something from you? Are they trying to manipulate you? Are they flirting with you? Trying to seduce you? Distract you? Outmaneuver you? Are they feeling guilty about something? Is there something to hide? You engage in self-talk, asking yourself these questions when you intuitively know something does not fit the situation.

This can also occur in a pastoral care situation. You discern that something is missing or is being left unsaid. The presenting problem—the "reason" the person gives for needing care—is not at the heart of the matter. You can always honestly ask: "I have a sense that there is something else troubling you. Is there anything else you might want to tell me? I feel I am missing something." You can put this in your own words. This query may help in trying to find the subtext, which is not dissimilar from the subtext in a mystery novel. Continue to listen, for there is certainly more to the story.

COMING ALONGSIDE

In the one-room schoolhouse, the instructor would sometimes come alongside a student working over a small chalkboard or reading in a book. "Coming alongside" of a person in need of our care is another way of reading between the lines, or being open to a subtext. Here is an illustration of that accompaniment in pastoral care.

Debbie had been director of Christian education in a church she had attended for twenty-four years. A couple of people were dissatisfied with her job performance and complained to the parish relations committee. The committee was quite affirming to Debbie, but the matter unsettled her. She suffered silently with doubts.

The senior pastor at the church noticed that Debbie was suffering "inner turmoil." Debbie writes: "He came along side of me, and provided me with a safe place to express my various emotions which included uncertainty, sorrow at the thought of leaving my church and friends, and anger at the 'complainers.' He allowed me to sit in his office and cry." The pastor was consistently supportive and asked questions to help Debbie think through her options and alternatives. He suggested steps to help clarify her call. Although her eventual leaving increased his workload, he stood alongside her and asked to be of help. After Debbie enrolled in seminary and received an appointment at another church, he continued to call to check on her and rejoice with her.[6]

This is "coming alongside" of a suffering person and offering attention and help when needed. It is like a teacher offering a way out of a mathematical impasse, never doing the problem for the student but instead helping to clarify possible steps toward a successful solution. Coming alongside of someone pastorally activates all aspects of the G-R-A-M-M-A-R in caring.

THE LANGUAGE OF THE CHURCH

Each culture has its own language or languages, and each language has its own grammar. The church operates with a language that includes words but is not limited to words. Prayer, song, Holy Communion, visitation, fellowship, and healing touch may involve the verbal, but these vehicles of care are never limited to words.

Kathie found this to be true when she visited Mary, a ninety-one-year-old resident of a Waterloo nursing home. Mary's angry daughter-in-law had informed Kathie, student pastor of Barclay Methodist Church, that the church had abandoned Mary.

Mary was very hard of hearing, and Kathie had difficulty communicating with her. That, coupled with Mary's short-term memory loss, made visitation a challenge. Mary's constant refrain was a signal to the student pastor: "I'm a lonely woman. So lonely."

Kathie and a commissioned lay pastor started taking communion to Mary. They included Mary's family. Mary was able to recite Psalm 23, pulling from her long-term memory. Bread and juice were shared, and a smiling Mary announced in a booming voice: "This is just like church!" Kathie, the student intern, learned to write all her visits on Mary's room calendar so the nurses could remind Mary that she had had visitors. Kathie learned to ask Mary about her seven sons; thus, there was never a lack of conversation. When Mary was distraught, Kathie put her hand on Mary's shoulder and offered a calming prayer. On days when Mary was not talkative, Kathie could always summon forth Mary's memory and strength to recite the Lord's Prayer.

When twenty-two members of Barclay Methodist Church showed up at Mary's bedside in mid-December for Christmas caroling, Mary could not be roused. Her hands, arms, and face were covered with large black bruises. She hadn't fallen; she was in the process of dying. The youngest child in the church, five-year-old Janie, held Kathie's hand. Kathie summarized: "As a church we gathered around Mary's bed and prayed the Lord's Prayer and then sang 'Silent Night.' I looked to see Janie's small little hand reach out and lay gently on Mary's gnarled bruised hand. I knew Christ was present in that room and in that touch."

On Kathie's last visit, Mary did not respond well. After prayer, Mary nodded and said: "That should do it." Mary died Christmas Eve morning, the day before her ninety-second birthday. During the funeral, one of Mary's grandsons gave this image to the congregation:

> "When I heard the pastor talking about Jesus coming to personally bring her [Grandma] home, I couldn't help but remember how Grandma loved to have her family come and visit. Do you all remember how she would call each of us over to her and put her hands on both sides of our face and pull us in and give us a big kiss whether we wanted one or not? All I can see now is Christ coming close to her and her reaching out to give him a big smacking kiss!"

Mary gave a picture of her faith in death.[7]

Images like this are also part of the language of the church. Sacraments, song, touch, prayer, Holy Communion, and the gathering of the priesthood of believers are certainly part of this language—a way of communicating God's presence and love and visibility. This language of the church of Jesus Christ is communicated in part through the grammar of caring.

At the close of the school year, a teacher often offers a summary of what has been accomplished. At the end of my class in foundations of pastoral care, I offer each student a black river rock and ask him or her to make it into a memorial stone. Paints and time to reflect are provided. This is reminiscent of the practice of the Israelites through the Hebrew Bible when a place or event was commemorated with "memorial stones" that were often piled up together.

One seminary student was later examined by his Committee on Preparation for Ministry and asked what he had learned about caring. The student said he had learned to walk "alongside of a person" and enter into their world, hearing them carefully. On his black rock, he had painted a big ear—to remind him of his need *to listen* to their grammar and their language.

Another student expressed himself through his poetry and used the image of the shepherd "coming alongside the sheep":

The Good Shepherd

Jesus you are the Lamb of God.
Guide me, lead me.
Help me to feed your sheep, as you have fed me.
When I was hungry, you fed me Your sacred holy Word.
When I was thirsty, you led me to the still waters.
When I was in prison, you opened the roof and set me free.
When I was afraid and broken, you walked gently beside me.
Help me to love your precious sheep as you have loved me.[8]

We are reminded that God listens to our language of need,
even those needs unexpressed and unknown. God's grammar of
care extends to us so that we might, in turn, better care for others.

• Question

Can you share an instance in which the love of Christ was communicated to you without words?

Chapter Three

THE PRISM OF PASTORAL CARE: SCRIPTURE REFRACTED

It was as if the seminary students in this foundational pastoral care course held up a prism through which the light of the biblical text offered different colors, displaying the splendor of our heritage.

In the one-room schoolhouse, the teacher would often ask, "What would you like to be someday?" In answering, students expressed goals for their lives. Then, perhaps, all the studying and "book learning" would make sense. Having a vision of the future gives energy to the efforts it takes to get there. Someone wishing to be a farmer or a doctor or a pharmacist or a banker benefits from a "picture" of what that will look like. I call this picture a "paradigm." In pastoral caregiving, it helps to have a picture of what being a pastoral caregiver looks like. For example, you may choose the image or paradigm of the shepherd. Or, you may choose a combination of several images or find a new model either in this chapter or in Scripture. Your task at the end will be to identify which model suits *you.*

In the one-room schoolhouse, simple objects were used as teaching tools or devices. There was no elaborate science equipment, so nature served as a science lab. An icicle hanging from the doorway, a drop of dew on the grass, or a droplet of rain caught in a spider's web could serve as a prism of light. Through this prism, many different colors could be seen, just as with the many-sided piece of glass we call a prism. If you hold a prism to the light, you will see various colors refracted through the one object.

Often, caregivers assume that only one image of the caregiver exists. Throughout history, the predominant image of the Christian caregiver has been that of the shepherd. The poem at the close of chapter 2 reflects this understanding. However, Scripture—when used like a prism of glass—can refract or reveal many different images of what caregiving can be. I had no idea how many until a crisis occurred one semester in which my students found an unexpected level of creativity and need. The goal of this chapter is not so much that you adopt one of the following example's images or paradigms in caring but that you find one that suits you.

THE CONTEXT

We were all vulnerable that spring, seminarians and professors and administrators alike. A widely respected and beloved seminary student was gravely injured in an accident. For weeks, she lay in and out of consciousness in the intensive care unit in Iowa City. The entire Christian community was absorbed in the suffering, then the loss. I believe our grief set the climate for the creativity that followed.

I had asked the seminary students in the required pastoral theology course to articulate a biblical paradigm for pastoral care. Many of the students came from rural backgrounds and planned to serve small, country churches in the Midwest. Some of the students, especially the Native Americans, later took positions in remote places in Alaska. The commonality that we shared was Scripture. Especially in this semester of our communal suffering, I asked the students to turn to the Bible for an image of pastoral care. I did not anticipate what they offered.

I remembered an art gallery in Geneva, Switzerland, that featured the works of Salvador Dali. The image that has lingered with me over three decades is that of Dali's "cosmic Christ," hovering over the earth, resting on a cross. Salvador Dali painted two similar images, meant to be viewed through stereo-optic lenses. The gallery in Geneva provided these lenses for the viewer. With the lenses, the two images of Christ were merged in such a way that he appeared to hover, and almost shimmer, over the earth.

I later acquired lithographs of these two images of the cosmic Christ. An optometrist came to my home to design glasses that would merge the two images into one. One of the prisms he brought actually multiplied the image of Christ into three. It was through the prism that I could see several images.

It was indeed as if the seminary students in this foundational pastoral care course held up a prism through which the light of the biblical text offered different colors, displaying the splendor of our heritage. Their images of pastoral care were artistic, diverse, and multivalent. And yet, as with the two images of Salvador Dali's crucified Christ, the prism of the biblical text also merged the distinct images into one—hovering over the world, with arms outstretched on a wooden beam, the cosmic Christ.

The students did not anticipate the manifold beauty of what they offered me, nor did they view themselves as wise and clever. They responded out of their desperate need. They offered me a new way of seeing, as with a prism. They had been gathered into a passion greater than their own. Fyodor Dostoyevsky wrote of such passion in *Crime and Punishment:*

> And when He [Christ] has finished judging all, He will summon us, too: "You too, come forth," He will say, "Come forth you drunkards; come forth, you weaklings; come forth you shameless ones!" And we will all come forth unashamed. And we will stand before Him, and He will say: "You are swine, made in the image of the Beast, with his seal upon you: but you, too, come unto me!" And the wise and the clever will cry out: "Lord! Why dost thou receive these [people]?" And He will say: "I receive them, O wise and clever ones, because not one among them considered himself worthy of this. . . ." And He will stretch out His hands unto us, and we will fall down before Him and weep . . . and we will understand everything."[1]

As you venture with passion into the ministry of pastoral care, you would do well to envision yourself as a caregiver. Your spiritual image of yourself may be altered by the context of your caring and that is to be expected. These steps may help as you start:

1. Acquaint yourself with the context.
2. Delve into Scripture.
3. Hold up Scripture as a prism.
4. Model your care.
5. Regard the refracted light of others.

THE CREATIVITY

Keep in mind that I had already introduced the students to the predominant image of the pastoral caregiver as Good Shepherd in Psalm 23. I had also broadened their base of knowledge with the priestly, prophetic, and wisdom models of caring ministry as well as that of the wounded healer.[2] I had never taught them to draw on one specific paradigm, yet I never envisioned the array that they discovered. One student saw pastoral care as being dynamic and varied because it is a way of being in relationship with others. Because of the many situations of life and the many possibilities for experience in relationship, he didn't believe that he could draw on one specific biblical paradigm; rather, he wished to blend together aspects of several paradigms to reflect the unique gifts given to each by God. He wrote: "This blending of paradigms not only reflects the individuality and variety of each of us, it also reflects the variety of situations we encounter in giving pastoral care."[3]

The blending of paradigms began to surface from both the Hebrew Bible and the New Testament. As the students delved into Scripture, they continued to grieve for their fellow student who lingered precariously on the threshold between life and death. Many of the students, even in the midst of their own suffering, were able to comfort those around them. Ruth's relationship to Naomi was used as a paradigm to support this pragmatic and hard caregiving: "In gleaning the fields day after day, Ruth displayed her love for Naomi in a way much stronger than words. This work was not only difficult and tiring, but involved potential danger for Ruth as well. Pastoral care will include, at times, sacrifice and risk."[4]

The seminary community became harbingers of mercy. A couple of the students identified with the Hebrew prophet Micah, who like them had come from the countryside. Plainspoken Micah's call to ministry was not accompanied by fanfare. He set a standard for pastoral care: do justice, love kindness, and walk humbly with your God. Another student found his own model for pastoral care in Matthew 25. This student wrote: "What is very clear is that in the end, either we fed the hungry or we did not. Either we clothed the naked, or we did not. Either we visited the sick, or we did not. As a Christian, I cannot read this passage as anything other than a call to works, or at least a call to the sort of faith that gives birth to works."[5]

THE GOOD SHEPHERD

During this semester of chaos, some students fell back on familiar images, but they did so from a deeper level of need. It was from this place of helplessness, I believe, that their old images took new forms. One such image of care was that of the Good Shepherd. Wrote one student: "Unfortunately, this image has become stereotypically pictured as a rugged, independent male who has the ability to care and tend the flock single-handedly."[6] The student observed that young, unmarried women were often (shepherds or) shepherdesses in the nomadic lifestyle of the early Israelites. Some examples include Jacob's wife Rebecca, Moses' wife Zipporah, and Solomon's reference to a young female shepherd in his writing *The Song of Solomon*. Shepherds were the wise elders of the community as well as young children. Thus the good shepherd paradigm must be seen in both male and female imagery and as a community responsibility incorporating all ages. Caring for the flock is not limited to a lone male sitting on a hillside. Young women were also shepherds.

In my own development of the good Samaritan parable in Luke 10 as a paradigm for pastoral care, the importance of distributing the responsibility in caring for the wounded by the side of the road is illustrated in the teamwork of the Samaritan, the innkeeper, and the beast of burden. During the semester of the crisis, I called for help to the American Red Cross. Outstanding therapists, clinical psychologists, school psychologists, and counselors trained in crisis care gathered from all over the city. They led support groups for spouses, children, and students. The director of the community mental health center talked to the students over a meal provided by a mainline denomination. The students saw the paradigm of the good Samaritan unfold in their midst. They as caregivers were cared for since many of them had responsibilities in churches and carried heavy responsibilities on weekends. Care of the self is modeled in Luke 10 as the caregiver or Samaritan finished his or her journey while exhibiting a balance between care of the other and care of self. If the Samaritan is seen as a representation of Christ, surely the wounded person experienced the loving gaze of God in the ministrations of the good Samaritan. Love of God, then, becomes interconnected with love of neighbor and self in the parable.[7]

In a further development of this paradigm, another student depicted women as "overextended caregivers" whose identity often disintegrates. However, when they learn to care for themselves, a change takes place that can be illustrated within the parable of the good Samaritan. This student wrote: "Using the paradigm of the Good Samaritan, I see the woman now changing from the wounded person to being the Good Samaritan. As a caregiver with no identity she is indeed the one lying alongside the road where all others in her life walk past her, never noticing she needs care. The really hard part is to get up off the side of the road and take the new place in life as the Good Samaritan. . . . When she becomes healthy, she can give care, but also include herself in getting care. She will give of herself to others and give of herself to herself."[8]

THE LONG JOURNEY

Days turned into weeks as the community continued to pray for the recovery of our student. It was not to be. There were times in the weeks that intervened that the grief grew so pervasive that we were almost immobilized. Almost—but the journey in caring continued. Another student discovered a relevant image of care in the walk to Emmaus: "Jesus' walk with two disciples en route to Emmaus offers yet another model for pastoral care. Jesus joined two people in their grief. He was with them as they traveled, asked a few questions, listened, shared information or facts, allowed for this information to be processed, waited for them to invite him further into the relationship and to discover truth on their own. Then, he knew when to leave."[9]

Seminary faculty preached sermons that extended pastoral care. Care was offered through the celebration of Holy Communion. The community gathered for the funeral service as the seminary choir, in which the student had sung, sat near the simple pine coffin. One student wrote of the apostle Paul as a model of pastoral care in the midst of farewells. At the end of Acts 20, wrote the student, "he is saying good-bye to all of the elders and people in the churches he visited. . . . Knowing he would not see this beloved church again in this life, he did two things for them: he preached the Word and celebrated the Lord's Supper. All his care for them centered in these two activities."[10] When Eutychus fell three stories out of the window during Paul's sermon, Paul embraced the boy, comforted the people, and claimed Christ's power over evil and death. During this most difficult service, we claimed Christ's victory over even this life of ministry cut short.

The end of the semester came and, with it, graduation. A master of divinity degree was awarded posthumously. The entire assembly stood in a memorial of silence. We lingered a little longer at the reception that followed. Then it was time to let go, not of the memories but of the support. One student used the relationship between Jonathan and David as an excellent example of rendering pastoral care. Jonathan knew that David would have to leave when King Saul got enraged. Although it grieved Jonathan deeply, although he was opposed to David's escape, he let him go. The student wrote: "While David is still with him, Jonathan walks a part of the journey with David, but then also knows that it is time to let go, and in so doing he empowers David to pursue the new course that God has chosen for him in his life."[11] This is what is meant by "coming alongside" of someone and offering a ministry of presence.

Multifaceted images of pastoral care have been offered in this chapter, from Micah to Paul, from Ruth to the shepherdess, from Jonathan and David to the walk to Emmaus, from Luke 10 to Matthew 25. This is an example of Scripture refracted into the many colors and hues and paradigms of care. What is important is that you choose a model for your caregiving. If one of the models presented here does not fit what God has called you to do, perhaps now is the time to explore Scripture to find one of your own. What kind of caregiver will you be when you grow into this kind of ministry?

• Exercise

Find an image of pastoral care in Scripture that suits you. Is there a person or model with whom or with which you can identify? Feel free to use one already mentioned or to select a new one.

> Samaritan?

Chapter Four

THE COMMUNITY AS CLASSROOM: AVOIDING COMPASSION FATIGUE

This last love, love of self, is the most difficult to remember as a caregiver.

Every teacher reaches a point of exhaustion, usually near the end of the day or near the end of the semester or school year. Both teaching and pastoral caregiving are professions of helping others. It is not uncommon to experience "compassion fatigue,"[1] a type of burnout or self-depletion. When this happens, the teacher or caregiver has given so much to others that there is little energy or compassion left over to give himself or herself.

An African American tells her own story. I first met her in an extension course I was teaching in the South. I was stressing the importance of taking care of ourselves as caregivers. This woman, whom I shall call Carolyn, wrote of a turning point in her life that some theologians call "a negative limit." In other words, Carolyn reached a place of awareness that revealed a "danger zone" she learned to avoid.

Carolyn's story unfolded. She was the model mother and wife, toiling into the late hours to provide for her family. She had the somewhat traditional marriage: she cared for the home and the children, including their schooling and their clothes. She shopped for the meals, prepared them, and cleaned up afterward. She and her husband both worked outside the home to provide enough income for their family of five. Carolyn rose early to shine her children's shoes, iron their school clothes, pack their lunches, and make certain they had a warm breakfast. In the evenings, she maintained order and cleanliness among the clan. She went to bed last and rose first. She ate the burned toast; she automatically took the smallest piece of meat or pie. Carolyn did this without thinking because she had learned this pattern of behavior from her mother, who had learned it from Carolyn's grandmother. This "selfless-ness" went back for generations.

One day, Carolyn, who was rarely sick, came down with a debilitating case of the flu. She had high fever, vomiting, chills, headaches, and fatigue. She collapsed in bed. The murmuring and complaining started. Where was dinner? Where were the clean clothes? Who would cook? And so on.

Carolyn lay in her bed unattended. Hours passed. Her fever was so high that she had a terrible thirst. She called out to her family: "Please, could someone bring me a glass of water?" No response. She summoned vocal strength and reiterated her request several times. Her family heard, but they did not respond. No one brought Carolyn a cup of cold water.

As she lay there ill, Carolyn reflected on all the years she had waited on her family like a servant and how now, in her sickness and need, no one—literally no one—brought her a cup of cold water. When Carolyn eventually rose from her sick bed, she vowed to be a different woman. She lived to change her life. She learned to care for herself, after having been in such an extreme situation in which she was neglected. She pulled back from her ministrations to her depen-dent family and shifted the dynamics. She ended up in my class "Pas-toral Care of Women" and studied for the ministry.

Women like Carolyn are finding a necessary balance in their lives by adhering to the paradigm or model of the good Samaritan. Do you remember the story?

THE GOOD SAMARITAN

There was a lawyer who tested Jesus with the question: "Teacher, what must I do to inherit eternal life?" The full account is recorded in Luke 10:25-37. Jesus asked the lawyer to look in the law. The law commanded the hearer: love God with all your heart, soul, and strength, and your neighbor as yourself.

Below is the commandment. First read it, and whisper or qui-etly mouth the last two words in brackets:

> You shall love the Lord your God with all your heart, and with all your soul, and with all your strength, and with all your mind, and your neighbor [as yourself]. (Luke 10:27)

Now reread the commandment and emphasize the last two words in brackets.

> You shall love the Lord your God with all your heart, and with all your soul, and with all your strength, and with all your mind, and your neighbor [*as yourself*].

I was raised on this verse from childhood, but I did not hear the last two words until I was in my late thirties. Seeing the command to love myself in Scripture was the mandate or permission I needed to do so. Those of us socialized like Carolyn to take care of others, whether as firstborn of the family or because we were women, have a tendency to neglect ourselves. I also find this tendency in caregivers in ministry, because we have not realized the interconnectedness of the three loves: love of God, love of neighbor, and love of self.

Following the lawyer's question and Jesus' answer is the parable of the good Samaritan. A man traveling from Jerusalem to Jericho was stripped and beaten by robbers. The poor sojourner was left for dead. A priest passed by without stopping, as did a Levite. But the least likely person to stop, a Samaritan, had pity and compassion for the beaten traveler and stopped to help. The Samaritan bandaged the wounds, pouring water and oil on them. The Samaritan enlisted the aid of an animal to transport the wounded to an inn. Then the Samaritan gave the innkeeper money to care for the wounded man.

How does this demonstrate love of self? you may ask. Travel with me farther into the narrative. The Samaritan left the wounded man with the innkeeper, finished his or her journey, and followed up with aftercare. The Samaritan not only paid the innkeeper but said that anything remaining as debt would be repaid upon the return visit. The Samaritan managed to care for the wounded man while finishing his or her own journey. By finishing the journey, the Samaritan exhibited self-care. By delegating the responsibilities in caring and relying on other professionals (i.e., the innkeeper), the Samaritan avoided compassion fatigue.

The statistics of burnout or depletion in ministry are alarming. In a 2002 study conducted by Austin Theological Seminary

(PCUSA) titled "Clergy Burnout Survey," 272 recent graduates of seminary were asked the following question: How often do the following situations create stress in your life?

Stressors	Very Often	Often	Occasionally	Rarely
Too many demands on my time	41%	33%	25%	1%
Feeling drained in fulfilling my functions in my congregation	21%	26%	39%	12%

This survey had a response rate of 59 percent (161 returned), with more women responding than men (54 percent women, 46 percent men). In another survey of Presbyterian clergywomen, 3,853 clergywomen were asked to rate fifteen issues of concern and indicate the importance of each concern using an intensity rating. Of the respondents, 1,404 rated the top two categories as "professional burnout" and "self-care."[2]

Issues	Intensity Rating	Importance of the Issue			
	4=major issue 0=not an issue	Major issue	Definitely an issue	Minor issue	Not an issue
Professional	2.01	442	550	252	87.5
burnout		33%	41%	19%	7%
Self-care	1.99	451	553	241	109
		33%	41%	18%	8%

This survey grew out of a concern over the decreasing number of women serving congregations and the increasing number of women leaving parish ministry.

Women have traditionally been socialized to care for others; that is, their main purpose in life is to provide for others. Thus, growing up in the South, I had always imagined women like the Samaritan, leaning over the needy or wounded, frozen in a posture of care for others. Now I see women and men who are caregivers as the journeying Samaritan, who indeed stopped to care for the sufferer but who also finished the journey, thus engaging in self-care.

We often think of the ordained minister as the Samaritan, following in the ministry of Christ, whom many commentators see depicted in the good Samaritan parable. Whether ordained or lay, any of us who undertake pastoral care in Christ's footsteps are susceptible to compassion fatigue. The parable in Luke 10 is timely because it illustrates the balance between self-care and care of others while giving us permission to distribute the load of caring with the "innkeepers" in our communities. It is out of love of God that we undertake this risky mission.

Situations utilizing "innkeepers" will be discussed more thoroughly in chapter 5. However, for our purposes here, some examples of "innkeepers" could include medical personnel, such as nurses and doctors, therapists, clinical psychologists, or facilitators of support groups such as AA (Alcoholics Anonymous), Bosom Buddies, and Resolve. Innkeepers could be social workers, staff at halfway houses or rehabilitation centers, staff and trainers at domestic violence prevention programs, and volunteers and trained professionals at rape crisis centers or child abuse prevention programs. Innkeepers could be pastors or laity, such as Stephen Ministers. Innkeepers could be hospice personnel or volunteers for Meals on Wheels. The innkeepers are as varied as the "inns" that support us in our caregiving to individuals in need. Sometimes the inns will be a Christian location or institution. At times, God will use institutions or organizations that are inclusive of Christians but not limited to Christians. For example, Alcoholics Anonymous is a support network that makes Christians feel welcome but is open to other faith orientations as well. God will ask us to work as a team with these "inns" and "innkeepers" who are ecumenical or interfaith or nondenominational. As long as the suffering person can feel safe and respected and encouraged in his or her own profession of faith, we as Christians should welcome the opportunity to network with other professionals as innkeepers.

TEACHER APPRECIATION DAY

When I was a single schoolteacher in Memphis, Tennessee, I often received twenty or twenty-five Christmas presents from my junior high students. I remember spending a couple of hours opening these gifts with my family watching. I felt very loved by those seventh and eighth graders. Some of the presents were homemade and others store-bought.

My most memorable gift was a homemade one: potpourri. A student had taken a lemon, poked it with cinnamon cloves, dunked it in some substance, let it dry, tied a ribbon around it and pronounced it finished. She had carefully placed it—the pot-pourri—in a box with tissue to cushion it. The box was wrapped very tastefully with a bright bow.

We all noticed there was a funny smell under the Christmas tree that year. We never could locate it until I started to open "the box." As I took the top off, I started to sneeze and gray fungus powder flew into the air around my family. I looked inside and found a decaying ball of fungus with a droopy ribbon and a card that said: "Merry Christmas, Miss Stevenson. You are a great teacher. I made this for you myself! It is to make your drawers smell nice. Love, Allison."

I knew this student as a caring, lovely, sensitive seventh grader. She had meant this gift to be beautiful. I never told her that her gift had died between the last day of school in December and Christmas Day. Nor did I tell her about the decaying condition in which I received it. I wrote her as grateful a note as the other children because I knew Allison had intended her handiwork to be "teacher appreciation."

Many schools today actually celebrate Teacher Appreciation Day or participate in local and national awards for their teachers. Our society is rightly recognizing the amount of energy expended in being a good teacher. You as a caregiver will also expend a great deal of energy, primarily in listening and in being with another person. You deserve appreciation, which can come in as many different ways as packages under a tree. However, as a caregiver, you will often be accompanying another person through suffering, transition, loss, pain, accident, or injury. Those for whom you care cannot be expected to express the thanks you surely deserve. The journey of care that you walk together may have ravines of rancor, detours of depression, and valleys of volatile emotions. There may not be "caregiver appreciation" on this concourse of caring. You will need to start with appreciation for yourself, which is another way of saying, "Love yourself." Following is an example of one woman's struggle to love herself.

Brenda, a woman in midlife, did not consider herself attractive in terms of looks or personality. She made a weeklong retreat with other seminary students. There was quite a bit of silent time at the retreat, during which she felt God very near. She walked the labyrinth, she wrote in her journal, she worshiped, she prayed, and she sang. One day, in the solitariness of her simple room at the Dominican retreat center, she was drawn to the mirror. She began to look at her face. And it was beautiful. She looked at the pores of her skin. Some were large and pocked from pimples of her youth. On that day, they were beautiful. She looked at the lines on her face. She smiled. They were smile lines. And they were beautiful. Even the age spots looked beautiful. Her eyes were a radiant blue; even the gray in her hair was a pretty color on that afternoon. Brenda wrote:

> As I looked at my face and caressed my skin, I was struck with a thought. It was God telling me, "This is how I see you. You are beautiful to me. What you don't like: your pores, your lines, your age spots are all beautiful to me." I couldn't tear myself away from the mirror. For once I was not looking at the mirror, hating my flaws. I was looking at myself through God's eyes. I was able to love myself as God loves me. I was seeing myself through God's eyes and for the first time in my life, I was beautiful. As I walked down the stairs to go for my hike, I thanked God that I am not beautiful by society's standards. I am just plain. Because I am plain, God has blessed me to see myself through God's eyes. And I am beautiful.[3]

In the 1950s, a major study was done of more than ninety theological institutions in the United States and Canada. Three theologians posed the following question: What is the goal of theological education? These men—H. Richard Niebuhr, Daniel Day Williams, and James M. Gustafson—discovered that the recurrent refrain of theological institutions was as follows: to foster or increase among people the love of God and love of neighbor.[4] Now, in the first decade of the twenty-first century, those of us teaching at theological institutions are alarmed by the dropout rates in ministry. It is time to add a third chorus to the earlier findings. The question to be asked: "What is the purpose of theological education?" The answer: to promote love of God, love of neighbor, and love of self.

This is also the goal of pastoral care. Of the three loves, love of self is the most difficult. As Brenda discovered, it requires seeing ourselves as God loves us. It then frees us to appreciate ourselves and to love ourselves in the way that God does.

THE RED DRESS

Every teacher has a favorite outfit, usually a comfortable yet flattering one. You can probably tell which one it is by how often it is worn. One of the most memorable stories I have heard was about a woman who never got to wear her favorite dress. The narrative is titled "Millie's Mother's Red Dress," a story about a red dress that hung in the closet as Millie's mother lay dying—"like a gash in the row of dark, old clothes she wore away her life in."[5] Millie listens to her mother describe this dress that she bought with a little extra money she saved. When she brought home the big box, Millie's father got angry and sarcastically asked if she was going to the opera. So Millie's mother never even put on the dress; she just put it on a hanger in the closet.

As she lay dying, Millie's mother recalled all the years she was the first one up in the morning, the last one down; she remembered taking the burnt toast or the smallest piece of pie so the others could have the best. She taught a lesson to her sons: "A woman doesn't even exist except to give." On her deathbed, her husband shook her violently and screamed: "What will become of me?" She had provided a free ride for everyone. Millie's mother asked one promise from Millie, and that was to *not* follow in her footsteps. The red dress hung in the closet as Millie's mother waited, as she had always waited, to take her turn in death.

Women who have been expected to care for others at the expense of themselves are learning to live a balanced life. They are wearing their red dresses. Women are learning this balance between care of self and other in a variety of ways. Yoga and Tai Chi classes are becoming increasingly popular because they promote the balance of energy and the centering of the body. Women and men are educating themselves on nutritional and healthy eating habits; exercise is becoming part of a daily routine. Support groups are being sought for affirmation, for fun, and for some form of healing. Women and men are becoming more involved as health care consumers. They are raising money for research, attending health fairs, and shopping around for health care providers. The church is also growing into a greater awareness that taking care of one's body, emotions, and mind is a part of responsible stewardship. Whereas the church has traditionally been noted for its care of the soul or spirit, it has become more aware daily of the care of the body and emotions.

As a caregiver, you have a biblical mandate to love yourself. This is not a selfish or narcissistic undertaking. It is a commandment that Christ has emphasized. Your lifelong task will be to discover how you can better love yourself. This may involve getting to know and accept your inner child, that part of yourself that was vulnerable when you were very young. Acceptance of your inner child may include looking at areas of woundedness or hurt that need further healing. Loving yourself could involve examining destructive patterns in your family of origin, the family into which you were born or adopted. Unhealthy patterns of interacting will most likely replay themselves in your marriage and in your professional relationships. Loving yourself may also entail developing an ability to say "no" to others. This, of course, is a means to achieve greater balance in your life.

In the foundational pastoral care course that I teach to all first-year seminary students, we spend a portion of one class going around the room with an exercise in saying "no." Students join me as we try to entice someone to take on more responsibilities. We can be very persuasive at times. However, in order for a student to graduate from the class, they have to form the word "no." It is humorous on occasion as we watch the lips struggle to form that most difficult word.

At the close of this chapter, you will find a sample of a journal page, which may help as you seek to achieve balance in your life between care of self and care of others. If you do not work toward a healthy balance in the three loves—love of God, love of neighbor, and love of self—the amount of suffering and trauma you will encounter in pastoral caregiving can be overwhelming and can cause an imbalance in your life.

In running a marathon, runners learn to pace themselves. In *The Ministry Marathon*, Tim Wright and Lori Woods maintain that the ministry is like a marathon.[6] When caregivers do not pace themselves well, they can collapse or fall out. Statistics in this book based on a survey of pastors reveal the following:

- 80 percent feel that pastoral ministry is negatively affecting their families.
- 70 percent say that their self-image is lower since they entered seminary.

One Lutheran minister, an actual marathon runner, talked about "hitting the wall" at mile twenty-three if not prepared: "To be in good pastoral condition, with plenty of reserve, requires plenty of good sleep, a regular exercise program, hobbies and passions outside of the church, whole and healthy family relationships, and a rich prayer and scriptural life. This conditioning has to become a way of life and not an occasional outburst of inspiration or motivation (no weekend warriors needed). As clergy, we are in it for the long haul and must learn to thrive and not just survive."[7]

A Methodist minister said: "I entered the ministry at the tender age of 20 years because I had an experience of the Holy while caring for a dying woman thereby feeling called to minister to the 'sin-sick' soul, yet I have never asked the question: how will my soul be cared for?"[8] A Presbyterian pastor confessed: "As pastors, myself included, we are notorious in running flat out to care for our congregations while we abuse, neglect, and torture ourselves into depletion. I speak for myself when I say, I rarely have time to read Scripture for my own personal well being."[9] These are words of warning from seasoned pastors, cautions that are important ecumenically for caregivers, whether lay or clergy.

GRADUATION

It is very important before you graduate from this chapter to the next that you have a clear plan of action regarding your style of caregiving. As mentioned earlier, the model of the shepherd has always been the most popular in the church. Another model for caregiving was promulgated by the late Henri J. M. Nouwen and termed "the wounded healer." The concept is based on an old legend in the Talmud, taken from the tractate Sanhedrin.[10] Rabbi Yoshua ben Levi came upon Elijah sitting at the entrance to a cave. Rabbi asked when the Messiah would come. Elijah told him to go and ask. "Where is he and how will I know him?" asked the rabbi. Elijah said he was sitting at the gates of the city: "He is sitting among the poor covered with wounds. The others unbind all their wounds at the same time and then bind them up again. But he unbinds one at a time and binds it up again, saying to himself, 'Perhaps I shall be needed: if so I must always be ready so as not to delay for a moment.'" Nouwen presents a caregiver as both the wounded minister and the healing minister, binding his or her wounds while still prepared to heal others.

Another model or paradigm in pastoral caregiving is that of the clown. This image was promoted by Heije Faber from Holland and by Seward Hiltner from Princeton. "The clowns remind us with a tear and a smile that we share the same human weaknesses. Thus it is not surprising that pastoral psychologists such as Heije Faber in Holland and Seward Hiltner in the United States have found in the clown a powerful image to help us understand the role of minister in contemporary society."[11] "Of the clowns, we say, 'They are like us.'"[12] As an example, a student pastor was making his evening rounds during Clinical Pastoral Education at a hospital in Wisconsin. He came across that dreaded sign: "Anyone entering, put on a gown and gloves." He seriously thought about skipping this presurgical patient who could have had a contagious disease. Instead, he donned the outfit. Upon entering the patient's room, he saw another man, the patient's husband, wearing a gown and gloves too. The lay minister introduced himself and added, "I see you're wearing a 'clown suit,' too!" This comment served as an icebreaker, and all three laughed. The visit ended with all three holding hands: one patient and two clowns in their suits.[13] Clowns cause us to laugh because they are like us.

To these three most widely used paradigms—shepherd, wounded healer, and clown—I have added a fourth: the Samaritan. Perhaps all four will be of help to you; perhaps a combination of two or three may serve your purpose. It is the good Samaritan who illustrates the care of self in finishing the journey while balancing care of the suffering other in the midst of this journey. In the "tyranny of the urgent," which we all encounter as sensitive Christians, it is a strong incentive to maintain a balanced life when we see such a life sanctioned by the one who epitomized the good Samaritan: Christ himself.

Christ was placed in situations of stress and was subjected to constant demands. In the Gospel accounts, Christ took time away from ministering and even found places of solitude. He had a group of disciples from whom he would also pull away at times. One classic book written about Christ's attempt to stay balanced in ministry is titled *Tyranny of the Urgent*.[14] The author points out that Christ did not heal all the sick in Palestine, nor did he feed all the hungry or free all the prisoners in the Near East. Even Christ was surrounded by the urgent demands that so often can tyrannize or paralyze us in ministry. Christ did not leave us with a model of meeting every need of every person whom we encounter. I am not saying that Christ could not have done this. Rather, I am stating that Christ's ministry did not model this.

As we are placed in situations of stress, we as caregivers will want to monitor the sources of stress in our personal lives. It may help to calculate the severity of psychosocial stressors upon you. The method for doing this has been provided in a manual used in the training of psychiatrists and other mental health workers and is reproduced in the wellness inventory at the end of this chapter.

Care of others will create its own stressors. A 2001 survey of 925 ministers revealed that the demands placed on them by parishioners take a toll. In answer to the question "During the past year, have you experienced stress because of the challenges you face in this congregation?" the responses were as follows:

Very often	21 percent
Fairly often	36 percent
Once in a while	40 percent
Never	2 percent
Not applicable	1 percent[15]

It is important as we come to the close of this chapter that you take a self-inventory of the stresses you already bear. It is even more important that you take a self-check to make certain you are receiving the support and care you need. Severe, extreme, or catastrophic stressors on you at this time will make it difficult for you to carry the heavy burdens of others while you are managing so many yourself. This is not to say that in the future or in another time period you could not be a caregiver. In fact, your own personal knowledge of suffering—in God's time—will make you even more compassionate toward others. If you do decide that God is calling you into this caring ministry at this juncture of your life, be alerted to the dangers of compassion fatigue. In order to avoid this malady, you will need to engage in teamwork with other helping professionals in the community. //

Remember to delight in yourself, for you are the delight of God! This is one of the reminders of Adolfo Quezada in his power-ful booklet *Loving Yourself for God's Sake!*[16] In God's love for you, you will find a model of the way you are to love yourself.

Stressor Scale

Acute events

Code	Term	Acute Events
1	None	No acute events that may be relevant to this disorder
2	Mild	Broke up with boyfriend or girlfriend; started or graduated from school; child has left home at eighteen
3	Moderate	Marriage; marital separation; loss of job; retirement; miscarriage
4	Severe	Divorce; birth of first child
5	Extreme	Death of spouse; serious physical illness diagnosed; victim of rape
6	Catastrophic	Death of a child; suicide of spouse; devastating natural disaster

Enduring Circumstances

Code	Term	Enduring Circumstances
1	None	No enduring circumstances that may be related to this disorder
2	Mild	Family arguments; job dissatisfaction; residence in high-crime neighborhood
3	Moderate	Marital discord; serious financial problems; trouble with boss; being a single parent
4	Severe	Unemployment; poverty
5	Extreme	Serious chronic illness in self or child; ongoing physical or sexual abuse
6	Catastrophic	Captivity as hostage; concentration camp experience[17]

• **Wellness Inventory**
Please fill out this wellness inventory to the best of your ability.
You do not need to use complete sentences. This is for you to keep
and to adjust from time to time. Remember that this inventory
will emphasize self-care of body, mind, and spirit. It is comparable
to the form you fill out in your doctor's office before your annual
checkup.

1. From elementary school on, we have learned about nutrition.
(Remember the pictures of the ham sandwich, apple, and glass of
milk?) What adjustments do you need to make in your diet?

2. How much exercise do you need each week not only to keep in
shape but to handle stress? How much are you getting?

3. How much sleep do you need each night? How much are you
getting?

4. Are you "burning the candle at both ends" (i.e., self-depleting)?
If so, what could be eliminated?

5. Is there at least one person (friend) with whom you can be yourself and reveal your fears and from whom you experience deep and
trustworthy acceptance?

6. Where is your support group? In the event of a personal crisis or
setback, who would constitute your sustaining circle?

7. How do you allow God or the Holy Spirit to fill you so that you
do not become depleted in caregiving?

8. Are you mindful of your own areas of growth that might benefit
from counseling or from spiritual direction?

9. Is there at least an hour a week that you have fun?

10. When was your last complete physical exam? Are you overdue
for one?

11. Do you have enough time alone (for solitude)?

Fitness Journal (sample page)

Date _____

1. What do I need to let go?

2. In this space (after letting go), what is the Holy Spirit trying to give me, as a child of God?

• **Weekly routine**
Physical exercise (Two hours per week minimum is recommended.)

Nutrition (This includes dietary changes and accomplishments as well as hydration, drinking five to six glasses of water per day.)

Play or leisure (Two hours per week is a minimum.)

Rest (How much sleep do you need each night? Have you made progress in allowing for this amount?)

Time alone (Were you able to spend time alone? How much do you need? Did you allow for this? Are you nurturing the artist within? Note: Every person has an artistic capacity, often expressed as the "artist child" within them.)

• **Biblical and theological insights that arose during the week:**

Chapter Five

THE OPEN CLASSROOM: PLACES OF CARE

*I approached the patient, now in a coma, and began
to sense a Third Presence in that room.*

In the 1970s, one of the most innovative concepts of teaching became "the open classroom," which was an environment of fluid space and learning. Some open classrooms have expandable walls or no walls at all. In this chapter, we will look at the most frequent places of care, spaces that are open to many emotions and an equal number of ways to learn.

DEATH OF A PARENT

Every person shares this common denominator: we all have parents. Some of us were raised by one or more birth parents; some of us were raised by adoptive parents, foster parents, or stepparents. Even those raised in a group home know they have birth parents. They may not know them, see them, or love them, but every child born is born of two biological parents. Even in this age of artificial insemination, every grown child knows there were two individuals who gave of themselves.

Most people experience a transition or passage at the loss of a birth, step, adoptive, or foster parent. It is not uncommon to hear, "It's not that I wanted him [her] to suffer any longer. It's just that I will miss seeing his [her] face." Most parents have been around since our birth. We have never known a time without them. Even if a geographical or emotional distance has occurred, parents precede us in a line of succession or genealogy. With their passing, we advance in the living lineage. We may now be at the head of the family. This realization, in itself, can be unsettling.

Even more traumatic is the death of a parent when the offspring is very young. Few sights are more wrenching than to see young children standing alone on the front row of a funeral. The trauma is increased if accident or injury or illness has claimed the lives of both parents. The sight of minors sitting at their parents' wake is almost unbearable. You as a caregiver will search for words yet find none that seem adequate. The hardest "work" will be to sit in silence and feel the depth of the pain. You may be the repository for some of the anguish, and perhaps for some of the anger and outrage too. You may hear confession, guilt, cursing, swearing, promises, or oaths. You may see outbursts of tears and wailing. To accompany a child in the loss of a parent is one of most strenuous journeys in your pilgrimage of care, one that is superseded only by accompanying a parent in the loss of a child. This is to journey to the abyss of hell and look over into the precipice of pain. It is at this precipice that Christ will hold onto you as you together hold onto the grieving. To face death is to face the last enemy.

When children, teenagers, or young adults face the loss of parents, it is best if there are caring relatives to step into the situation. It is also the role of the church family to provide nurture and guidance to these "orphans." In fact, it is a biblical mandate to do so. There may be financial repercussions; here is where members of the church could help. There may be other times when helping professionals from outside the church are needed, particularly if the child exhibits "acting out behavior," such as delinquency, or shows signs of prolonged depression. If a child or young person is a danger to himself or herself or to another, we may break confidentiality and enlist help.

With the awareness today of sexual abuse, incest, and domestic violence, we should be forewarned as caregivers that, in rare instances, a young person may be relieved after a parent's death, if that parent has been a perpetrator of such violence. Usually, this is a complicated grief with a variety of emotions. As a care provider in these instances, be alerted that the grief may be tricky, slippery, or convoluted back on the self. This is an occasion to seek the "innkeepers" and "inns" of care discussed in chapter 4, such as a rape crisis center, local council on child abuse, or domestic violence prevention program in your town. At these places, "innkeepers" can either help or provide referrals.

Grief usually runs through stages. Dr. Elisabeth Kübler-Ross presented some of these stages as shock, denial, anger, bargaining, and eventual acceptance.[1] These stages do not necessarily follow one another neatly. Grief can also come with other losses in addition to death. As Wayne Oates pointed out, grief and separation are constant companions in this journey of the life cycle, from birth to death.[2] Divorce is one such loss.

DIVORCE

Divorce is the death of a marriage. To make matters worse, sides can be taken in divorce. Your agility as a caregiver will be tested as you sidestep the blaming and crossfire that can occur between divorcing partners. You are called in not to take sides but to be a "nonanxious" presence in the mix of emotions. Divorce can activate all the stages of grief as well as add betrayal and an outrage over injustice to the mixture.

Divorce can be devastating to children in the marriage as well as to extended family members. If a third party is involved, it can be easy for that third person to be seen as the cause for the dissolution of the marriage. Normally, however, there were preexisting deficiencies in the marriage or areas that went unattended. Even so, a third party can be used by the dissatisfied partner in the marriage as a rationale or a lever to break up the marriage. This is not always the case, of course, but it is wise to remember.

The death of a marriage is described in a poem brought by a man named Marv to his therapist:

> Their wedding picture mocked them from the table, these two
>   whose minds no longer touched each other.
> They lived with such a heavy barricade between them that neither
>   battering rams or words nor artilleries of touch could break it
>   down. Somewhere between the oldest child's first tooth and
>   the youngest daughter's graduation, they lost each other.
> Throughout the years each slowly unraveled that tangled ball of
>   string called self, and as they tugged at stubborn knots, each
>   hid his searching from the other.
> Sometimes she cried at night and begged the whispering dark-
>   ness to tell her who she was. He lay beside her snoring like
>   a hibernating bear, unaware of her winter.
> Once after they had made love, he wanted to tell her how afraid
>   he was of dying, but, fearful to show his naked soul, he
>   spoke instead of the beauty of her breasts.

She took a course on modern art, trying to find herself in colors
    splashed upon a canvas, complaining to the other women
    about men who are insensitive.
He climbed into a tomb called "The office," wrapped his mind in
    a shroud of paper figures, and buried himself in customers.
Slowly, the wall between them rose, cemented by the mortar of
    indifference.
One day reaching out to touch each other, they found a barrier
    they could not penetrate, and recoiling from the coldness of
    the stone, each retreated from the stranger on the other side.
For when love dies, it is not in a moment of angry battle, not
    when fiery bodies lose their heat. It lies panting, exhausted,
    expiring at the bottom of a wall it could not scale.[3]

As caregivers, you will contend with the desire to "fix" a stale or
stalemated marriage. If you are unable to assist a troubled marriage, then you will need to refer the couple to trained marriage
and family counselors or therapists. The national network of
American Association of Marriage and Family Therapists can be a
source of "innkeepers."

When a family is under stress, such as in a divorce, the family
members fall back on familiar patterns, often dynamics they have
learned in their family of origin or their family of development.
Family members will seek to enlist your support or "vote." They
will want you to be on their side of "the wall." One dynamic that
we learn to avoid as caregivers is that of triangulation, a movement
to engulf you in an emotional triangle. For example, let us say one
partner in a marriage has an affair. That partner leaves. The remaining partner and the child at home try desperately to have you side
with them in an emotional triad called a "triangle" in family systems theory. Your role will be to listen and help them navigate the
dangerous deadlock of divorce, not to become involved in a tug-
of-war or a round of power play. You will hear many theological questions, most notably, "According to the Bible, isn't divorce
wrong?" You will want to formulate a grace-filled response to this
query, especially when the one asking is in an abusive, threaten-
ing, or deadening marriage. One viewpoint has been expressed by
Stephanie Paulsell: "Fidelity is wielded like a weapon when it is
used to keep someone in an abusive or deadening relationship."[4]

What can you provide to a parishioner who decides to go through the loss called divorce? Sarah, now in her sixties, tells of her recovery from divorce and of the role another church member played for her.

> Divorce was a major landmark in my life's journey. In 1972, I was 34 with three children aged 12, 9, and 5 when my husband decided he did not want to be married anymore. 1972 was an awful year for me. A church friend had me (and often my children) to dinner once a week all that year. Frances and her husband took me to dinner and to concerts. She visited, she called, she loved. I said, "Frances, I can never repay you for all you are doing for me." She replied, "You'll give to someone down the road. That's the way life is." My gifts of love and nurturing, the gifts I bring to the church, exist because of all the Franceses God has given me through the years.[5]

She visited. She called. She loved. You may not be able to do exactly as Frances did. It may not even be appropriate for you to do so. For example, there may be boundary issues if you are clergy and the divorcing person is laity. There may be sexual or gender considerations that bear on which actions you undertake to show concern and care. For example, if you are a single female, your solicitous outreach to a divorcing male may be misconstrued as sexual overtures. This can work in reverse, male to female, as well. The person undergoing divorce will be quite vulnerable and subject to both misperceptions and misconceptions. This is unfortunate and unnecessary, but true. Thus, although your kindness may take a different form from that of Frances, you can still visit, call, and love. Divorce is a lonely, disconcerting, unsettling, and chaotic time. Compassion shown by members of the church family can have life-altering implications down the road.

MISCARRIAGE, STILLBIRTH, AND THE LOSS OF A CHILD

There is a fate worse than one's own death, I believe. That is the loss of a child. When I was editing a trilogy of books on women's issues in pastoral care, I found one noticeable gap. I tried to tell myself there was no one who came forward to write the missing chapter.

That unwritten chapter was on child loss. I tend to believe it was because the topic was simply too painful to sustain. Even to imagine the loss of a child is more than the rational mind can tolerate.

I have often said, "If I should ever lose one of my children through death, please send me someone who understands the pain." Translated, that means, send me someone who has also lost a child.

As a pastor, although this may not be your situation, you will still need to be a first responder to the grieving person or family. However, it is advisable to arrange for a lay caregiver who has experienced this devastating loss to follow up with visits. This would need to be someone whose grief is not raw and fresh, because encountering the similar situation could trigger unresolved grief in the caregiver. This would overload the care-giver and care-receiver. In a way, the loss of a child will always be somewhat unresolved. It is a pain that lessens in time, although it never goes away completely. It is a tragic truncation of life that a parent learns to live with in due time.

National support groups that undergird grieving families also exist, such as The Compassionate Friends, SHARE, Candlelighters Childhood Cancer Foundation, and RESOLVE. Most cities have a local support group, although a parent with raw grief might hesitate to go right away. This grief in the loss of a child cannot be rushed; it can only be supported. Support groups have substantiated the realization that those who have previous and similar losses can be of most help.

Miscarriage and stillbirth are the loss of a child. More and more birth mothers and fathers are asking that this early loss be treated with the same compassion as the death of a full-term baby or a viable newborn. Pastors should be prepared for the request to baptize a fetus or a stillborn baby. This possibility needs to be thought through at the beginning of ministry, preferably while still in seminary. If you have theological hesitations or ecclesiastical policy or polity issues, it is best to find a colleague in ministry who can fulfill the wishes of the bereaved. Often, hospital chaplains are prepared for these emergencies. Such a chaplain could be your "innkeeper" in this situation. Please do not stand in theological judgment of a grieving birthparent who makes this request. If you cannot perform the baptism, stand with the chaplain or pastor or priest or rabbi who can do so. Advocate for the parents. As an ordained pastor, you will most likely be asked to perform a funeral for a stillborn baby. Be also prepared to perform a funeral for a miscarried baby. The hospital staff is becoming more prepared for the grief of miscarriage. Sometimes, photos will be taken, articles of clothing will be given as remembrances, or loving rituals will be performed. Lay caregivers can respond with acts of kindness and companionship just as they would with the loss of an older child.

I recently had a Stephen Minister call me about a parishioner who was undergoing infertility treatments. The request reminded me that surgeries that unite an egg and a sperm, such as in-vitro fertilization and Gamete Intrafallopian Transfer, create their own unique losses when the fertilized eggs fail to implant in the uterus or when the embryo ceases to develop. The national group RESOLVE has specialized on these complicated, devastating losses and offers support on the local level. Again, people who are experiencing this gynecological roller coaster of emotions will need one another to help remind them of their normalcy. Help a hurting person find a support system!

One last word of caution: when we think of the loss of a child, we often picture the biological child, the physical offspring of a couple. Those who have adopted children are also parents. They are parents who have often gone through a great deal to have a child. They have taken on a huge responsibility and are generally deeply invested in their children. The loss of an adopted child may be a more complicated loss. For example, the parents may wonder: "Would she/he have been better off with the birth parent?" Or they may blame themselves: "If I hadn't let her go on that camping trip, the accident wouldn't have happened." Any parent can engage in retrospective thinking, but an adoptive parent has usually promised in a special way to care for this child. Maybe it was not a vow or formal promise, but it is surely an interior one. The loss of a child is the loss of a life not lived. You will be asked to walk through the valley of the shadow of death. You will be expected to proceed as a "nonanxious presence" in an atmosphere of chaos. Remember to walk with God, the one who knows what it is like to lose a child.

DEPRESSION

There are three types of depression that you may encounter in your caregiving ministry.[6] In all cases of depression, it is imperative that a physician evaluate for possible causes and contributing factors. Thus you will want to make certain that the person you are talking to has had a recent physical.

In the instances of bipolar depression, often called manic depression, the person will exhibit extreme mood swings—from a high mood of elation to a low period of depression with low energy. Someone suffering bipolar disorder will need to be in the care of a skilled medical physician, and medication will be required to regulate the highs and lows, or the pendulum swing of moods. The manic phase may take many forms using high energy levels; some in a manic phase will shop excessively or start up numerous businesses at once or keep so many "balls juggling in the air" that there is a frantic or frenzied feel about the activities. In the low periods, which typically include depression, despair, and even hopelessness, a person can be a suicidal risk. This is why medication is used to stabilize the chemical imbalance that usually underlies bipolar disorder. A physician, preferably a psychiatrist, will prescribe the medication. A lay caregiver can befriend someone suffering manic depression but can never *treat* the person. A minister, however, can offer skillful care and counseling as a member of a support team that includes a doctor who both treats and dispenses the medication. The mild form of bipolar disorder is called *cyclothymia* and may or may not need medication.[7]

A second type of depression, known as major depression, has been described as falling into and staying in a "black hole." A precipitator or precipitating event, such as the loss of a child or a job, may catapult someone into a major depression. Major depression can also be caused by a chemical imbalance in the body and thus require medication to regulate the imbalance. Sometimes, hospitalization is also required. Again, major depression needs medical supervision by a depression specialist. Clergy are not trained in seminary to professionally manage this type of depression in a parishioner, nor are clergy licensed to medicate. Even if a lay caregiver is a physician trained to do these things, in the role of lay caregiver it would be wise to place the person suffering major depression under the medical care of another. In this way, the lay caregiver is freed to give supportive companionship to the sufferer while maintaining a healthy boundary. The teamwork we have discussed earlier comes into play as various members of the team fulfill their needed roles. The third type of depression is a mild, low-lying depression called *dysthymia,* or depressive neurosis. You may hear the phrase, "I feel blue." This form of depression can be tied to a situation or circumstance, a loss or grief, or a disappointment or change. It is to be taken seriously. Dysthymia responds most readily to compassionate outreach, skilled listening, catharsis or the expression of feelings, and companionship through the difficult period. Lay caregivers can also provide a supportive presence for a person suffering from dysthymia. Sometimes, medication will also be indicated or needed or professional therapy or counseling will bring healing and relief. Again, this illustrates the importance of teamwork in caregiving.

Before closing, let me mention postpartum depression, which can follow childbirth. It is not uncommon for a mild depression to follow childbirth. After all, the mother's body has had major trauma, even perhaps surgery. Hormones are adjusting. Family is gathering. Life is radically changing with the arrival of a helpless infant. However, if the mother's mild depression or "blues" lasts more than two or three days, it could be postpartum depression, a clinical syndrome that necessitates the diagnosis of a physician with possible intervention. Usually, postpartum depression will be spotted by nursing staff or doctors in follow-up visits. Nevertheless, it is important for family, friends, pastors, and other caregivers to be cognizant of the mother's mood after delivery and to be in conversation with medical personnel.

Depression is a slippery malady to diagnose. This is why we as caregivers work closely with the medical profession to make certain that depression is properly diagnosed and treated. In all forms of depression, pastoral caregivers can work as part of a team with medical personnel to give holy and holistic care to the sufferer.

HOSPITALIZATION AND SURGERY

Not all hospitalization requires surgery, of course, but all surgery requires hospitalization. With current medical advances, more and more patients undergo same-day surgery, which means a very short hospital stay or time in a surgical center. The common denominators in all lengths of hospitalization and all forms of surgery are still fear of an unknown outcome, discomfort in an unfamiliar environment, a sense of powerlessness and lack of control, and invasion anxiety. A person who is a patient in a hospital will be very vulnerable and, most likely, welcoming to your care.

If you have ever been a patient in a hospital or surgical center, it would help to remember your feelings. If you can remember and name your feelings with honesty, that will be the best teacher of how to equip yourself to engage with the sick, injured, or hospitalized. It is not your place to tell the patient about your experience. It is your role to claim your own experience by naming it, accepting it, and using it within yourself to be more receptive and perceptive of the care receiver.

The founder of psychoanalysis, Sigmund Freud, wrote at length about castration anxiety among men. At its root, castration anxiety is the fear of having something significant cut off or taken away from the body. However, castration anxiety has also been extended to fear of losing authority or self-respect or one's identity. In a hospital or surgical setting, the fear of waking up and finding a limb or body part missing or the fear of mutilation can occur. One of Freud's followers, Karen Horney, adapted Freud's theory to women. As a feminist, she wrote of women's fear of invasion, a fear based on their anatomical structure (i.e., the vagina or uterus), which can be penetrated. Invasion anxiety can certainly involve rape or incest; it can also be extended to mean psychological violence done to a person's inner sense of self.

I mention invasion anxiety in this section because it helps to explain, in part, the fear of hospitals and surgery. Many procedures, whether they are insertion of tubes, needles, or IVs, are invasive to the body. Chemotherapy, radiation, dialysis, and other procedures are intrusive. They may be necessary and life-saving, but they are nevertheless foreign to the natural organism.

As caregivers, we would do well to acknowledge that a hospital or outpatient center may not feel like a safe place to the patient. This is all the more reason why you as a caregiver will represent the familiar: the familiar face, the known community of believers, the trusted helper. When you walk into the room or the clinic, you are the nonanxious presence in the midst of all the instruments and gadgets. You are the oasis of calm. You symbolize the fact that God is, somehow, in control. Surrounding you is the aura of the known, the safe, and the noninvasive. It is an honor for God to call you into this situation; it comes with great responsibilities. Here are a few things to learn:

1. Be respectful of the "gatekeepers" in the hospital or surgical center. The book *The Pastor and the Patient,* by Kent Richmond and David Middleton, offers more detail.[8] In brief, you will need to have good relationships with those in authority in the hospital. The parking lot attendant will know whether reserved places are available for chaplains, priests, and pastors. You will want to check in at the reception desk and identify yourself. In this way, you will not be disruptive in case there are strict visiting hours or a "no visitors" policy for the patient. The persons with the most power are the nurses, especially the one at the desk in the ward to which you are headed. Identify yourself as a pastor or Stephen Minister or lay minister; ask how the patient is doing, and then inquire whether you might make a *brief* visit. All of the people I have mentioned will be more eager to accommodate you if you treat them, and the patient, with this kind of respect. They will be more willing to open "the gates" for visitation.

2. Much of your role will be listening. You will be there to create a safe, inviting space for the patient to ventilate or express his or her feelings. However, some statements you might make are potentially harmful. These inappropriate comments are labeled "bromides" and can be deadly.[9] Let me give you a few. You visit a woman who has just lost a child through stillbirth. She is weeping when you enter the room. Meaning to be positive, you say, "Don't cry. I am sure you can have another one." This comment is disastrous on two accounts. First, tears are healing. Even Jesus wept. Second, although it may be physiologically true that this woman can have another child eventually, to express this is to deny her pain over losing *this* child. Always accept the patient's emotion. Never deny or belittle or minimize

it. This woman's grief is real and valid, and it needs to run its course.

Here is another example of a bromide: A father loses his teenage son, who had many developmental difficulties. Perhaps the son had been in trouble with the law or had been involved in drugs. The bereaved father is indulging in "what ifs" or "I should have…." You feel his pain, and you blurt out this bromide: "Don't torture yourself like that. He's better off in heaven." This is a disastrous comment because it makes a parent feel like he shouldn't be grieving so. A parent who has lost a child is entitled to grief.

3. Do not overtax the patient. Better to stay too short a time than too long. If you don't know whether to say something or not, don't. Your presence and the fact that you took time to come will make the most lasting impression.

4. Remember that you represent the church, the body of Christ. If you are ordained, it may be in accord with your ecclesiastical tradition to offer the sacrament of Holy Communion. The sacraments and rituals of the church have a transformative power anywhere, but especially in the chloroform corridors and cubicles of a clinical setting. You might take in cards from other church members. Be creative in ways that the church community can be represented, such as standing outside a window with lighted candles, caroling during the Christmas holidays, and caring for the family of the patient. The hospital is a holy place, and God will lead you and be with you through the labyrinth of hallways.

Let me close with a story. You will see the influence of one interim pastor on a seriously needy family. Donna's daughter was seriously injured in an automobile accident in a major city halfway across the country. Both of her lungs had collapsed, a collarbone was broken, her liver was lacerated, and she suffered a spinal cord injury that has rendered her, to this day, a paraplegic. Donna and her husband caught the night flight out and found their daughter unconscious in the intensive care unit of this unfamiliar hospital on the East Coast. Within ten days, the daughter underwent three surgeries. Donna and her husband lived in a hospitality house.

Every night, their interim pastor, Greg, called and left a message. Donna stated, "I knew he would take our calls any time of day or night, which was a great comfort."[10]

Three weeks later, the family returned to the Midwest by air ambulance. The daughter faced more complications and surgery. At the end of her ability to cope, Donna called the pastor. Even though it was late and a long drive to the hospital, the pastor, Greg, asked whether he could come sit with the family during the daughter's abdominal surgery. The family protested his coming at first, but he insisted that he really wanted to be there. Greg showed up, gave hugs, listened a lot, and brought news of the congregation. Donna wrote: "It was a relief to be able to talk to someone about our fears and hopes, and as I recall, there were even a few jokes and the first laughter in weeks." After the surgery, Greg took the parents into the hospital chapel, where they held hands and prayed. Donna wrote:

> He had turned an evening of worry and stress into a warm caring circle of shelter. Looking at what made this event so effective, I was struck at the time, and still am, by the amazing gift of his quiet presence and full attention to our needs, late on a Wednesday evening, staying with us past midnight. Though our daughter graduated from college last Saturday and is looking forward to a spring internship, summer job, and (hopefully) graduate school in the fall, those dark days are still full of difficult memories. However, the night that Greg sat with us during her last surgery remains in our memory as a respite of calm and comfort.[11]

Prayer, the sacraments, and your presence as Christ's representative will create that calm and comfort.

Chapter Six

THE OPEN CLASSROOM: MORE PLACES OF CARE

They were looking at me, but they were seeing Jesus.

LONELINESS

Loneliness is a feeling of isolation and disconnectedness that can affect and infect any age or gender or nationality or socioeconomic class. Loneliness is pervasive in North American society. In fact, when Mother Teresa of Calcutta spoke to a graduating class at Harvard University, she spoke of this poverty of spirit called loneliness. Mother Teresa's work in India and throughout the world with the Sisters of Charity focused on material poverty but she also recognized the poverty of loneliness, which can be a painful ailment of the soul.

We tend to think of the solitary individual in a deserted situation as lonely. However, many lonely people can be found in crowds, in families, in college dorms, and in bustling workplaces. Loneliness can be caused by dislocation, from moving off of one's land or away from a familiar and cherished place. Loneliness can be caused by a sense of disconnect, which occurs when it seems there is no one who knows the real you and, more frightening still, no one who cares to know the real you. Loneliness can occur in a marriage when the partners in the marriage are living separate lives and cease to share. Loneliness can occur at any school age, particularly when a student is excluded from circles of peers. Loneliness can also be brought on by illness.

I am going to use two stories of loneliness here because they illustrate how the church may step in to connect with the isolated individual(s). The first instance occurred in a nursing home as a young licensed Methodist pastor struggled with pastoral care. The pastor perceived herself as having no skills for relating to elderly people. It was the day to offer communion, and she planned familiar hymns, a short Bible passage, and a sermon. Most of the residents did not know their names and could not carry on a simple con-versation. Senile dementia or Alzheimer's disease had taken a toll on them. Some of the residents could not see. The pastor was very uncomfortable—until the singing started. She wrote later: "Women that could not see could sing 'Amazing Grace!' Some of them could not carry a simple conversation, yet their spirits said The Lord's Prayer. They couldn't remember what they did two hours ago. . . . But they could sing the refrain of 'In the Garden.'"

When it came time for communion, the Protestant pastor was again fearful. She had been informed that most of the women were Roman Catholic and used to a priest. However, when she said, "This is the body of Christ for you," the women looked at her but did not see her. She wrote: "Their eyes were very clear, and I believe for that moment, their minds were clear. They were looking at me, but they were seeing Jesus. It was a holy moment." Thus, a com-munity was formed around the hymns, the prayers, the Eucharist (Holy Communion), and the biblical stories of the church. It is one way to break the isolation of aging.[1]

In the second story, a seminary student writes of a lonely man carrying a tedious, cumbersome, and secret burden. When there is no one with whom to share, life can be very solitary. This young man was a "hippy" with unkempt hair down to the middle of his back, several days of whiskers on his face, and a disheveled look about him. He became a guest in the house of the Lord on a cold March day. He wore a flannel shirt and no coat. He gave a short introduc-tion, looking around at the "old, wrinkled people that sat around him." He imagined their critical eyes upon him. So he looked down at his Bible and not at the aging "pillars of the church."

The seminary student wrote: "Some of the old men, sitting by their wives, smiled and squeezed their spouse's hand. In the way that only people that had lived together for most of their lives can, they said without ever speaking a word, 'Remember when we were young? My hair was a little too long and cold weather never both-ered me, either.'"

Meanwhile, the young man lamented that he had come to this church where the pastor was his best friend's father. How could he possibly share such a burden with these people with whom he had nothing in common? As the seminary student wrote: "The older people, through years of living and being sensitive to the prompting of the Holy Spirit, could tell that the young man carried a secret, heavy burden. Many started to pray, 'Dear Lord. Give us the words to say if words need to be said. Give us the wisdom and opportunity to listen if words need to be heard. Let us minister to your child today.'"

The young man squirmed as the Bible study proceeded and as the prayer requests were taken. Slowly, the burden crushing his heart started to shift. He could not suppress it any longer. His facade dissipated, and the burden came out, "not in great detail, but with much sobbing and cleansing. There was also a great peace that young man had never known. No words were spoken. A withered hand was placed tenderly on the young man's heaving shoulders. Instead of the judgment of strangers that the young man expected, he experienced the love of dear brothers and sisters in Christ."

There were tears all around that night, because the people in that circle had had their own hearts broken a time or two in "servant living." "They didn't know the situation, and didn't have to, for behind those wrinkled eyes beat hearts of gold." One of the members said a prayer that the young man remembers to this day. "I see in [this young man] the spirit of a young Timothy." Words of acceptance, love, and commission. It was the circle of Christ. In the young man's words, "Christ made real." This young man was the seminarian before me, and this exit from loneliness was his most meaningful experience of pastoral care.[2]

A prayer into the woundedness. A withered hand on heaving shoulders. A circle of comfortable silence when words are not needed. A word of encouragement. Christ made real.

RELOCATION, MOVING, AND HOMESICKNESS

Relocation to a new school, a different part of town, or an unfamiliar geographical region often results in disorientation and dislocation of one's sense of identity and "at-home-ness." We all desire to be at home with ourselves, at home with one another, at home with an accepting family. Moving—whether from one business to another or from one town or state to another—can precipitate such a sense of being lost or disconnected. Many of you reading this will not be in your hometown or city of birth. Chances are that you have moved a great deal. You may recall how bleak the holidays can be without old friends or family nearby, and how we long to be with old friends and just "pick up the conversation where we left off" because they know our history.

The church has been likened in Scripture to a healthy, functional family. The imagery of Ephesians, in particular, talks of God as father, children, sons and daughters. However, the imagery in Ephesians 1 assumes an adopted family is the norm. Christians are adopted as sons and daughters by God with Christ as firstborn of the family. There is a secured inheritance, guaranteed by the Holy Spirit. The rest of the book of Ephesians tells how to live as children of God.

One theologian has rightly asked: "Where is the mother of the family in Ephesians?"[3] Because the cult of the Great Mother was so popular in the Mediterranean region at the time this New Testament book was most likely written, it can be surmised that the author of Ephesians veered away from the mention of Mary, mother of God. As you will recall, Paul and his followers spoke out against the goddess Artemis, the polymastoid, or many-breasted, goddess of fertility. This is one manifestation of the cult of the Great Mother.

Nevertheless, even with the absence of a mother, the family imagery is used in the book of Ephesians.[4] The metaphor of adoption also occurs in Galatians and Romans. The Gospel of John refers to a second birth as an alternative metaphor for illustrating the family of faith. My point here is that the church is intended to function as a healthy, nonabusive, and accepting family. In a family constructed through adoption, differences must be accepted for that family to be functional. Genetics and biology will not be the tie that binds. Instead, in a family of faith formed by God's gracious adoption, it will be Christ who makes us relations.

When a person is dislocated geographically, reassigned, stationed away from home, or otherwise raising a family away from relatives, he or she desperately seeks belonging. This is where the church is called to make a difference, to welcome the stranger. This acceptance of differences and this hospitality to other adoptees are a major mission of pastoral care. As Matthew 25:35 reads: "I was a stranger and you welcomed me."

WIDOWIIOOD

One founder of the modern-day pastoral care movement was Seward Hiltner, whose book *Pastoral Counseling* has become a classic.[5] Hiltner had his students write up "contact reports." Following is that of a student named Peter Manning, who was asked to make a house call on a recent widow named Mrs. Tompkins.[6] Mrs. Tompkins had not shown much grief at her husband's funeral.

Manning approached the big house on a huge lot. In the rear of the house, there was a separate apartment. Manning found Mrs. Tompkins with a mop in her hand, in working clothes, cleaning out this addition to the main house. Her eyes were bloodshot, and she had a cold.

Much of the ensuing conversation was about the separate wing of the house. It seems that Mr. Tompkins was something of an amateur architect and had designed it. Manning tried to suggest the possibility of Mrs. Tompkins renting this wing out and other such "helpful" comments. Mrs. Tompkins sobbed, put her head down, and moaned, "I'm so lonesome. My husband was all I had. Oh, it's terrible with him gone." Feeling uncomfortable, Manning tried to soothe her and to "fix" the situation—and, in Seward Hiltner's opinion, missed her completely. Manning himself later observed: "I didn't get down to her basic troubles at all."[7]

Marriages come in many shapes and sizes, as do divorces and widowhood. There may even be some widows or widowers who sense some relief when their partner passes, since the death of a spouse in later years often follows the ravages of illness and aging. However, the entrance into widowhood typically is a major life transition and can be a devastating passage. Somehow, the image of Mrs. Tompkins cleaning away in an appendage to her home, working feverishly with blood-shot eyes, has situated itself in my memory. There is no way to "fix" this pain. However, there is a way to function as a family of faith to respond to the plea: "I'm so lonesome."[8]

FAMILY CONFLICT

Every family will undergo some degree of conflict in their life together. However, there are serious degrees of conflict that we can attempt to understand through the lens of a theory called family systems. Developed by Murray Bowen and his followers, this system has proven quite useful in training chaplains and pastoral counselors.

An overview will have to suffice here, but a more detailed description and application has been offered by Ronald Richardson in *Creating a Healthier Church*.[9] The central thesis is that every family constitutes a system. In that system, each member plays a role. Some roles are healthier than others. For example, the eldest child will often be the achiever, the responsible one. This can result in pressure to overachieve or overfunction. Firstborn children are commonly perfectionists and often find themselves in highly responsible vocations like ministry. Firstborn children can slip into the role of a savior figure. On the other hand, the youngest child can easily play the clown or the entertainer. Some of the pressure is off when the last child is born into a family. The parent(s) are more relaxed; they have been through the routine before and thus can afford to lighten up on the youngest. These are only two of the many "scripts" that children and parents can play. Most of this "acting" is, of course, subconscious.

Most pastors and lay ministers will not be trained to do family therapy or to engage the issues in a seriously troubled family. Let me offer two examples.

Sue's most meaningful memory of pastoral care occurred when she was sixteen. She describes herself as a youth at risk. Her parents were very professional and functioned highly in the church. As Sue comments: "Mother was a teacher and a disciplinarian. She was angry with me because in her eyes I was not working up to capacity."[10] Years later, as an adult, Sue was found to have attention deficit disorder and learning disabilities. However, back in the days when this sort of testing was not offered, Sue was seen as having a "bad attitude." Sue adds: "A bad attitude was dealt with harshly in my family."

Sue's family took in over thirty foster "brothers"—that is, adolescent male juvenile delinquents. The church viewed her parents as noble and saintly. However, Sue and her biological siblings suffered under the strain of so many foster children in the home. Sue described some of the foster boys as "nasty and abusive." She was angry with her parents because her family felt splintered.

One day a youth leader in the church sat down beside Sue and said: "It must be difficult being [her mother's name]'s daughter."

Sue described this moment as "the flood gates opened." She had found one person who understood "how awful it was to be me." As the youth leader listened, Sue felt heard. She was accepted. She also knew her comments to the youth leader would be kept safe. She wrote: "His acceptance of my perspective and feelings about my family without judgement was one of the ways I began to understand that God loves me even when I am not likeable. He acknowledged me as a whole person who was experiencing my parent's gift to the world in a much different way. He gave me permission to feel and have thoughts that were not what I perceived as Christian."

I doubt that the youth leader in that time period had the lens of family systems theory. He may have intuited that Sue's mother was perceived as an overfunctioner while Sue was seen to be an underfunctioner. He may have guessed that Sue was scripted to play the role of "the lost child" or "the troublemaker" or "the angry, un-Christian child." This would be compared to the selfless dedication of the noble and Christian parents, at least within the family system. What the youth leader managed to do was to step outside the closed family system and offer a word of understanding and acceptance to the trapped child Sue. We can make this move without being well-versed in clinical studies of pathology in families.

The second example occurred in a supervisory setting in the training called Clinical Pastoral Education. Some seminarians are required to undergo this training while others are given the option. On this occasion, a Lutheran seminary student named Kathy was disclosing her deepest thoughts and feelings in a group of peers. Her supervisor reached out to hold her hand. It was the first time this had ever happened to Kathy in a nonromantic way. When she finished telling her story, the supervisor asked her to close her eyes and take a deep breath. He asked: "How old are you right now?" She started to cry and stated, "Five years old." He continued to hold her hand as she wept.

After some time, her peers responded with comforting words. She was surprised by her male peers' reaction because it was especially gentle and tender. One of the male peers was asked to speak to her as if father to daughter. Kathy experienced God's healing presence in that moment. Some days later, she opened her Bible to this passage in Isaiah 41:13: "For I, the Lord your God, hold your right hand; it is I who say to you, 'Do not fear, I will help you.'" She recalled her supervisor. As she wrote: "God was clearly present to me through his actions, just as God continues to guide and support me each day."[11]

Your role is to be a supportive presence. It is not your job to replace a parent, a spouse, a grandparent, or other relative. However, you may be used by the Holy Spirit to help heal a wound or help fill a gap in the development or nurture of a person. Boundaries must always be maintained between you and the care receiver so that the care receiver may heal properly as a separate self. This is an instance when an "innkeeper" may be needed, such as a marriage or family therapist. If a wound is very deep, especially if incest or sexual abuse has caused it to fester, professional help will be necessary.

ILLNESS OR INJURY

With illness or injury comes the loss of our sense of mastery and control. Illness and injury bring a sense of powerlessness to our well-being. This is only accentuated when we are in an unfamiliar setting. For example, Brian's father suffered a massive heart attack while hunting elk with his son in the Sierra Madre Mountains of Wyoming. The father was flown from one hospital to another and ended up in a hospital in Lincoln, Nebraska, not his hometown. He was there two months. One day, Brian entered the hospital room as his father got a phone call. At the end of call, the father remarked with a tear in his eye, "She has been so kind to me, and I have never met her." He was referring to the new pastor in his hometown church. This call and others like it offer a connectedness to those disoriented by illness or injury.[12]

In other situations, it may be possible for a pastor or lay caregiver to travel to the location of the ill or injured. In less populated regions of the country, it is also possible to activate a network of caring through hospital chaplains and pastors who live locally. One seminary intern living on Kupreanof Island, ninety miles from Juneau, Alaska, was unable to pay for the flight into Juneau to visit a parishioner who was hospitalized there. The student intern called the parishioner, initiated a village ecumenical prayer chain, and then asked a retired Presbyterian minister living in Juneau to call on the parishioner in the hospital. The student wrote: "He was a part of my 'team' for pastoral care."[13] Retired pastors, elders, and deacons are excellent resources for your caring ministry.

It is difficult to be prepared for illness and injury because each has so many forms. They also have an equal variety of responses. It is wise to be prepared for the anger that can accompany such setbacks in life. You may be the recipient of anger that is unintended for you personally. You need to be prepared for the wellspring of fury that can arise when a person loses control of his or her life. That person will be extremely vulnerable and exposed, and a form of regression or childlikeness can occur. You may witness outbursts of anger. Remember that this anger has nothing to do with you. Your ability to understand that and receive the expression of anger will be a great ministry in itself.

Of course, there are also instances of great heroism and faith among those who are suffering illness and injury. Some people model a way to face the final enemy, death, with such courage that we as caregivers become the beneficiaries.

I will close with an instance of pastoral care given to a man with lung cancer because this case demonstrates the multiplicity of ways a congregation can respond with care. A Methodist minister was approached by an elder with news of an unchurched family in desperate straits. The family was not active in any church in town. Nonetheless, they had approached various churches and been turned down by all—except this last Methodist congregation.

The forty-year-old father had lung cancer. Suffering the side effects of chemotherapy, he had had to quit his job. The mother, a day-care provider, had also left her job to tend the husband full-time. The family had liquidated their savings and been denied assistance by the county. They had filed for Social Security disability benefits, but the paperwork was slow. They fell behind on rent, with no money for gas or other needs.

For six months, beginning in August, 2000, the Methodist congregation helped with physical and material needs and became a caring presence through phone calls and visits. Parishioners offered to babysit the children (ages four and one) so the mother could get away for some time alone. The family was included in worship and church activities. At Thanksgiving, the ailing father asked for help to travel with his immediate family to a large family reunion in another state. The father had neither a trustworthy car nor the money for gas. The church provided both. The family returned on the Monday following Thanksgiving. On Wednesday of that week, the Methodist pastor—off at seminary classes—was called. The father had died. The pastor returned to perform the funeral while the congregation continued to support the wife and children. It was two more months before Social Security checks arrived, and in this interim, the church provided.

In April 2002, the Methodist minister baptized one of the children and presided as the mother took membership vows in the church. This true and recent account is, to me, an instance of irresistible pastoral care when offered by such a loving congregation.[14]

• **Exercise**
More than ten different scenarios of care have been presented in this chapter. Pick the one situation that would be the most difficult for you. Discuss that with your peer group. Be honest with your fears and hesitations. Be open to encouragement and acceptance from the group.

If we are honest about our worst-case scenario and prepare ourselves for it mentally and spiritually, we will be more relaxed in what God brings our way.

Chapter Seven

AN ALPHABET OF GRACE

In God's presence, I was all I ever wanted to be.

Often, on the last day of class, a teacher will attempt to offer a summary of all that has preceded during the year or semester or quarter. It is not uncommon for the teacher to offer closing thoughts or to remember "essentials" to be shared before parting. As a teacher, I always feel both anxiety and anticipation on the last day of class. I realize that the members of that particular class will never be assembled in that same way again. I also anticipate that unique "learning community" pouring out into a larger context around them and blessing others with their wisdom.

Writing this last chapter fills me with similar anxiety and anticipation. I am eager to impart a few last pointers. I also trust that you will seek additional knowledge and skills in areas in which you discern God's leading. In the notes at the end of this book, you shall find more resources for your ministry. This has been a basic offering, hence the title: *A Primer.* Originally, the book developed out of a pastor's request for a resource to encourage lay caregivers who may have only two or three days for foundational training.

In the one-room schoolhouse of my great-grandmother's era, two other items would have been prominent: an abacus or counting device and the students' lunch pails. I would like to close with these two images as they relate to pastoral care.

THE ABACUS

Before the adding machine and the calculator, there was the abacus, a primitive wooden structure used for mathematics. The abacus consists of a wood frame with movable beads or balls on wires. These beads slide back and forth to illustrate subtraction and addition in teaching arithmetic. The abacus is a device of certainty, because 2 plus 2 always equals 4, and 10 minus 5 always equals 5. These equations and others like them are predictable. They follow linear thinking with quantifiable results.

The ministry of pastoral care follows no such predictability. In fact, the most commonly asked questions that you will encounter among those who are suffering and burdened are these: "Why is this happening to me?" "How could a good God allow this [evil] to happen to me?" "How can this innocent child suffer?" "Why would these good people suffer?" There will be no logical answers to this questions, which in theological circles fall under what we call the question of theodicy. How can a loving God allow horrible things to hurt people? How does this logically follow? What sort of skewed equation is this?

There is no abacus in agony. Yet you will be asked these heart-wrenching questions. Please be prepared to receive them. Notice that I did not say, please be prepared to answer them. Sometimes there will be no answer at all.

In *When Faith Is Tested: Pastoral Responses to Suffering and Tragic Death*, Jeffrey Zurheide presents five possible frameworks from which to respond.[1] A deterministic framework tries to offer solace with the words, "It is God's will" (that someone is suffering). The didactic approach conveys the idea that God is teaching something through the suffering. The athletic answer portrays suffering as training, testing, or strengthening experiences sent by God. The disciplinarian framework suggests that God as parent is punishing or chastising for wrongdoing. The fifth framework offered by Zurheide is a struggle with the question of theodicy resulting in a sense of God's mystery and incarnational vulnerability. It is the latter that Zurheide suggests is most workable. Using the theological language offered by Karl Barth in his *Church Dogmatics*, Zurheide focuses on God suffering with us. Through the incarnation, an omnipotent God became flesh in the person of Jesus Christ, who lived on this earth: "Thus, as Jesus was rejected, God was rejected; as Jesus wept, God wept; as Jesus experienced profound suffering, so also God experienced the same."[2]

Let me offer an example. Suzanne writes of a time when she could not even mouth the words, "Why, God?" Her father died of a massive heart attack the day after Christmas in 1987. A friend made the trip to her house and sat there. Suzanne wrote: "She was just as uncomfortable as I was. She did not know what to say, and I could not say anything either. But in between silences, she said to me, 'I don't know what I would do if I were in your place.' That was enough for me to know that she cared and understood my pain."

Suzanne described her friend as a woman raised in a family of many brothers, a young woman who was comfortable working in the fields alongside them. She was not at home in a woman's world. When Suzanne later became acquainted with Scripture and the joy of studying the Bible, she came to realize how much this visit of outreach had ministered to her: "So her outreach to me at the time of my father's death is something I will always cherish. It was not in the words she said, but it was in the sitting and sharing with me my discomfort of grieving that I have learned that it is in the silence that one is most comforted."[3]

If her friend had made a cause-and-effect statement (e.g., "He just wore himself out caring for others"), there would have been no comfort. If her friend had chosen an "it could have been otherwise" statement (e.g., "If he had only gone for a checkup"), there would be guilt and retrospection. If her friend had used a biblical platitude (e.g., "God didn't cause him to die; it is just sin and evil in the world"), Suzanne's anger toward God could only have been intensified for she would be left with an impotent God.

The friend was genuine and did not make up answers to a question that baffles the most astute theologians. Why would a good God allow loving people to suffer? The friend shared the discomfort of grieving and understood the pain.

Death is the final enemy to face in this life. Christ stands with us as we sit—even in silence—with those who face this reality. It is Christ who will have the last word, even to the question of theodicy.

PRESENCE

A chief skill in pastoral caregiving is that of listening—to the silences, to the words, to the pain. This is a skill that will come to some more easily than others, but I do believe it can be learned.

You may be wondering whether there is a time for words of guidance, exhortation, or discipline in the ministry of caring. Certainly, there will be occasions that call forth those responses. Sermons, Sunday school classes for all ages, vacation Bible school, Bible studies, and conferences are all settings for verbal teaching. However, you will note that in many settings that call for pastoral care, a care receiver will be unable to absorb very much cognitively. This holds true not only for occasions of shock and sadness but for celebrations of joy as well.

Unfortunately, as a caregiver, you will be called upon for assistance most often in situations of stress, grief, loss, sadness, anxiety, and illness. Think for a moment of the lists of joys and concerns that are included in the worship bulletin, the church newsletter, or the Sunday service. What is the proportion of joys to concerns? Overwhelmingly, the concerns outweigh the joys. This will also be true in your ministry.

You may be called upon for guidance or exhortation or discipline in your ministry of pastoral care. However, in my experience, you will be sought out most for your nonanxious and pastoral presence, for your companionship, for your prayers, for your nonjudgmental listening abilities.

A seminary student wrote of the night her uncle committed suicide. Her grandparents (i.e., the parents of the deceased) were visited by their pastor, who had the difficult role of being the person sent to tell her grandparents that their son had died. She wrote: "My knowledge of this event is through my grandfather, who relayed the story to me about a year ago, which reveals the deep impression that was made by the minister's pastoral care. When the minister had finished telling my grandparents what had happened, my grandfather was understandably very upset. He expressed his emotions verbally, using many words and ideas not usually considered to be appropriate for use around clergy. In the face of this, the minister simply listened and accepted my grandfather's response."

The grandfather later felt ashamed for his behavior and expressed wonder that the minister did not judge him for his behavior. The grandfather realized that the situation had nothing to do with the minister, that the suicide was not the minister's fault. The student concluded: "I think the minister's willingness to receive my grandfather's anger without placing blame or retaliating, is an excellent example of meaningful pastoral care."[4]

THE LUNCH PAILS

The distances were often long to the one-room schoolhouse, particularly in areas of farmland, prairie, or swamp. Students brought their midday meal in a lunch pail or tin bucket of sorts. In winter, it was important to keep the food warm. Sometimes, the food pails were placed on or near the coal stove until the noon break, when students would eat together.

Christ has provided such a meal for us in the midday of our ministry. The common meal called Holy Communion or Eucharist is our break from expending so much energy. It becomes our time to take in nourishment through the body for the soul. Christ presides as teacher at this meal, as Christians gather in his name to eat and drink. Without this meal, we should not try to carry on in ministry.

This sacrament is at the heart of pastoral presence. We mingle in Christ's presence and leave better equipped to bear Christ's presence in the world. We offer up our fears and anxieties at the common table; thus we can begin to understand the possibility of a "nonanxious presence" in caregiving. We receive care from Christ at this table and replenish ourselves to better care for the world. We receive not only the bread and wine but the love and forgiveness to continue in ministry. The meal in the midday of ministry reminds us that those with whom we minister are sinners like us, in need of the warmth of absolution. As we approach the common meal around the presence of Christ the host, we are gathered together with the cloud of witnesses (Hebrews 12:1-2), men and women of faith who have preceded us into the full presence of Christ. Thus, not only are we encouraged by our own personal mentors in the faith who have crossed the threshold between this life and life eternal, but we are surrounded by those designated as saints in the history of the Christian church: John Chrysostom (who described pastors as "physicians of the soul"), Mother Teresa of Calcutta, John of the Cross, Catherine of Sienna, Thérèse of Lisieux, Oscar Romero, Howard Thurman, Dietrich Bonhoeffer, and so many others. This cloud of witnesses who are continually in holy communion with Christ encourage us in this journey of caring.

I do believe skills in ministry can be learned and enhanced by practice just as material is learned and practiced in the one-room schoolhouse. We must not neglect, however, the holy camaraderie of the midday meal, midway between what we start and what God will someday finish.

HOLY CAMARADERIE

A Swiss woman once recounted her "near-death" experience. She saw herself proceeding through a dimly lit tunnel and approaching a warm light. This light became more intense after she left the tunnel and slowly moved up a hill. Eventually, she realized she was approaching the throne of God. She went willingly and joyously forward into what she described as an antechamber. She told me: "As I imagined approaching the antechamber to the throne of God, I was bathed in grace. I knew in that instant I was all I ever wanted to be." Although she ceased breathing on the operating table, she regained consciousness and had amazing recall of the surgeons' conversations during her surgery. She also described her near-death experience with convincing certainty. Most importantly, she used an alphabet of grace: "In God's presence, I was all I ever wanted to be."

Pastoral caregivers are schooled in a holy classroom. Christ is our teacher or *rabboni*. We hear many sacred stories, such as the one recounted by the Swiss woman who was resuscitated on the operating table. Because some of the stories and situations are filled with pain, we learn to take care of ourselves, to love ourselves, as demonstrated in the parable of the good Samaritan. As you remember, the Samaritan in this parable managed to care for the wounded traveler by the side of the road while finishing his or her own journey. The Samaritan learned to find another helping professional, the innkeeper, to tend to the needs of the wounded. In this way, the Samaritan engaged in teamwork and activated a community of caring through the use of the inn. As pastoral caregivers, we shall at times confront situations that warrant specialized helpers or referrals, for example, persons suffering from major depression, bipolar disorder, suicidality or homocidality, sexual abuse, rape, or incest. For all of these situations, there are trained professionals to help. Referring a "traveler in need" to one of these professionals is an act of strength and a sign of wisdom.

In the Lukan parable, the Samaritan offered excellent aftercare by returning later to check on the wounded traveler and to offer financial resources. The fact that the Samaritan finished his own journey to Jericho, the fact that he balanced care of self with care of the other, might at first glance look like the Samaritan gave only "second best." However, this respectful love of self interconnected with love of neighbor is exactly what Jesus, the Great Samaritan, needs. The distribution of responsibility, the teamwork, is what Jesus desires. No one person, no sole minister, is to be overladen. This model of caring offered by the Great Samaritan can be heard in the schooling of the soul as a universal language with an alphabet of grace. //

We do not often think of innkeepers as significant team players. Yet, if we recall the narrative of the nativity, the birth of Christ, we remember that one very significant innkeeper in Bethlehem found room for two tired travelers. One traveler in particular, a pregnant woman, had a great need. She needed a place to sleep because she was near childbirth. In making way for this weary traveler, the innkeeper made room for Christ.

This has been the great reversal in the familiar story of the good Samaritan. Commentators have always made the Samaritan the focus. Yet Jesus tells this story in Luke 10 to a lawyer who is trying to trick him. In answering the lawyer's question, "Who is my neighbor?" Jesus gives the parable of the good Samaritan (Luke 10:25-37). The surprise at the end is that the innkeeper made room for the distressed traveler at the inn. The narrator of the parable, Jesus himself, knew what it was like for a traveler not to have room at the inn. Earlier in Luke's Gospel, we read: "And she [Mary] gave birth to her first born son and wrapped him in bands of cloth, and laid him in a manger, because there was no place for them at the inn."

I write the ending to this book a week before Christmas. In the Midwest there is a version of the nativity story with an unanticipated conclusion.[5] It is a true story about a nine-year-old named Wallace Purling. He was in the second grade that year, although he should have been in the fourth. He had difficulty keeping up, was a little slow and clumsy but was also very kind. The kids tried to exclude him from their games, but Wally hung around, ever the protector of the children at risk.

Wally so hoped to be a shepherd with a wooden flute in the nativity play that December. Miss Lumbard, however, assigned him a minor speaking part, that of the innkeeper. Wally got caught up in the timeless story unfolding on the stage as he stood, mesmerized, in the wings.

When the time came, Joseph tenderly guided Mary to the door of the inn. Joseph knocked hard on the plywood, and Wally the innkeeper was there waiting. Wally tried to sound brusque when Joseph asked for lodging. "Seek it elsewhere. The inn is filled," said Wally as he stared straight ahead.

"We have asked everywhere in vain. We have traveled far and are very weary," Joseph tried again.

Once again, a stern-looking Wally reiterated the fact: there was no room in the inn.

"Please, good innkeeper, this is my wife, Mary. She is heavy with child and needs a place to rest. Surely you must have some small corner for her. She is so tired."

Wally relaxed his stiff pose and, for the first time, really looked at Mary. He paused so long that the audience began to get nervous.

The prompter from the wings whispered: "Begone!"

Wally repeated the whisper: "Begone."

Joseph sadly put his arm around the pregnant Mary; she rested her head on his shoulder as the two slowly moved away. The innkeeper did not move. He stood transfixed in the doorway of the cardboard inn. His mouth opened, his brow furrowed, and his eyes filled with tears. And suddenly this Christmas pageant took an unexpected turn.

"Don't go, Joseph," Wally called after them. "Bring Mary back." Now Wally Purling's face shone. "You can have my room."

This school pageant is still being debated in parts of the Midwest. Some say it was ruined by Wally Purling. Others say it was true Christmas. I believe it was a metaphor of pastoral care at its finest, for pastoral care is making room for life's weary traveler and, in doing so, discovering Christ in our midst.

NOTES

Chapter 1. The One-Room Schoolhouse

1. Rob Brink, unpublished manuscript, Foundations of Pastoral Care course, University of Dubuque Theological Seminary, 2004.

2. Ibid.

3. Howard Stone, *Crisis Counseling*, rev. ed., Creative Pastoral Care and Counseling Series (Minneapolis: Fortress Press, 1993).

4. Peggy Ann Ellingson, unpublished manuscript, working title: "Living in a Fish Bowl: Jesus Did It, So Can You."

5. This episode came from the video, "At a Loss for Words: How to Help Those You Care for in a Miscarriage, Stillbirth or Newborn Death Experience" (Brewster, Mass.: Paraclete Press Video Production).

6. Amy Johnson, unpublished manuscript, Foundations of Pastoral Care course, University of Dubuque Theological Seminary, 2004.

Chapter 2. The Grammar of Care

1. Nelle Morton, *The Journey Is Home* (Boston: Beacon, 1985), 127–28.

2. Riet Bons-Störm, *The Incredible Woman* (Nashville: Abingdon, 1996), 11.

3. Paulette Klimson, unpublished manuscript, Foundations of Pastoral Care course, University of Dubuque Theological Seminary, 2002.

4. Gary McAlpin, unpublished manuscript, Foundations of Pastoral Care course, University of Dubuque Theological Seminary, 2002.

5. Howard Stone, *Crisis Counseling*, rev. ed., Creative Pastoral Care and Counseling Series (Minneapolis: Fortress Press, 1993), 75–77.

6. Debbie Pimm, unpublished manuscript, Foundations of Pastoral Care course, University of Dubuque Theological Seminary, 2003.

7. Kathie Jackson, unpublished manuscript, Foundations of Pastoral Care course, University of Dubuque Theological Seminary, 2003.

8. Tom McLaughlin, unpublished manuscript, 2004.

Chapter 3. The Prism of Pastoral Care

1. Fyodor Dostoyevsky, *Crime and Punishment* (New York: Signet Classic, 1968), 33.

2. Charles Gerkin, *An Introduction to Pastoral Care* (Nashville: Abingdon, 1997), 11–21.

3. David Poust, unpublished manuscript, Foundations of Pastoral Care course, University of Dubuque Theological Seminary, 2000.

4. Anonymous, unpublished manuscript.

5. Brian Jones, unpublished manuscript, Foundations of Pastoral Care course, University of Dubuque Theological Seminary, 2000.

6. Mary Anne Conklin, unpublished manuscript, Foundations of Pastoral Care course, University of Dubuque Theological Seminary, 2000.

7. Jeanne Stevenson-Moessner, "A New Pastoral Paradigm and Practice," in *Women in Travail and Transition: A New Pastoral Care*, ed. Maxine Glaz and Jeanne Stevenson-Moessner (Minneapolis: Fortress Press, 1991), 203.

8. Sylvia Larssen, unpublished manuscript, Foundations of Pastoral Care course, University of Dubuque Theological Seminary, 2000.

9. Tom C. Shinkle, unpublished manuscript, Foundations of Pastoral Care course, University of Dubuque Theological Seminary, 2000.

10. Tracee D. Hackel, unpublished manuscript, Foundations of Pastoral Care course, University of Dubuque Theological Seminary, 2000.

11. Gregg Pusateri, unpublished manuscript, Foundations of Pastoral Care course, University of Dubuque Theological Seminary, 2000.

Chapter 4. The Community as Classroom

1. Kate Jackson, "Compassion Fatigue: The Heavy Heart," *Social Work Today*, March 24, 2003, 21–23.

2. "Clergywomen's Experiences in Ministry: Realities and Challenges," Advocacy Committee for Woman's Concerns (ACWC), March 2002 survey, p. 22, table 2.

3. Brenda Whitford, unpublished manuscript, January Term Retreat, 2003.

4. H. Richard Niebuhr, *The Purpose of the Church and Its Ministry* (New York: Harper and Row, 1956), 31.

5. "A Feminist Perspective: Implications for Therapists," video (Topeka, Kans.: Menninger Video Productions, 1983).

6. Tim Wright and Lori Woods, *The Ministry Marathon* (Nashville: Abingdon, 1999), 14.

7. Marggi Pleiss-Sippola, unpublished manuscript, doctor of ministry seminar, 2004.

8. Sarah Rohret Odoom, unpublished manuscript, doctor of ministry seminar, 2004.

9. Linda Philabaun, unpublished manuscript, doctor of ministry seminar, 2004.

10. Henri Nouwen, *The Wounded Healer: Ministry in Contemporary Society* (Garden City, N.Y.: Image Books, 1972), 81–82.

11. Henri Nouwen, *Clowning in Rome: Reflections on Solitude, Celibacy, Prayer, and Contemplation* (Garden City, N.Y.: Image Books, 1979), 2–3.

12. Ibid., 2.

13. Dennis E. Govier, unpublished manuscript, Foundations of Pastoral Care course, University of Dubuque Theological Seminary, 2003.

14. Charles E. Hummel, *Tyranny of the Urgent* (Downers Grove, Ill.: Inter Varsity, 1967; rev. 1994), 6–9.

15. U.S. Congregational Life Survey, May 2001, Appendix B: Ministers of the Word and Sacrament, Presbyterian Church USA, The Presbyterian Panel, B-12.

16. Adolfo Quezada, *Loving Yourself for God's Sake!* (St. Meinrad, Ind.: Abbey, 1991), 69.

17. *Diagnostic and Statistical Manual of Mental Disorders*, rev. 3rd ed. (Washington, D.C.: American Psychiatric Association, 1987), 11.

Chapter 5. The Open Classroom: Places of Care

1. Elizabeth Kübler-Ross, *Death and Dying* (New York: MacMillan, 1989).

2. Wayne Oates, *Grief, Transition, and Loss: A Pastor's Practical Guide,* Creative Pastoral Care and Counseling Series (Minneapolis: Fortress Press, 1997), 33.

3. Author unknown.

4. Stephanie Paulsell, *Honoring the Body: Meditations on a Christian Practice* (San Francisco: Jossey-Bass, 2002), 29.

5. *In Her Own Time: Women and Developmental Issues in Pastoral Care,* Jeanne Stevenson-Moessner, ed. (Minneapolis: Fortress Press, 2000), 1.

6. Christie Cozad Neuger, "Women's Depression: Lives at Risk," in *Women in Travail and Transition: A New Pastoral Care,* ed. Maxine Glaz and Jeanne Stevenson-Moessner (Minneapolis: Fortress Press, 1991), 156–57.

7. Ibid., 157.

8. Kent D. Richmond and David L. Middleton, *The Pastor and the Patient: A Practical Guidebook for Hospital Visitation* (Nashville: Abingdon, 1992), 72–76.

9. Howard Stone, *Crisis Counseling*, rev. ed., Creative Pastoral Care and Counseling Series (Minneapolis: Fortress Press, 1993), 43.

10. Susan LeFeber, unpublished manuscript, Foundations of Pastoral Care course, University of Dubuque Theological Seminary, 2003.

11. Ibid.

Chapter 6. The Open Classroom: More Places of Care

1. Brenda Whitford, unpublished manuscript, Foundations of Pastoral Care course, University of Dubuque Theological Seminary, 2002.

2. Geoff Snook, unpublished manuscript, Foundations of Pastoral Care course, University of Dubuque Theological Seminary, 2002.

3. Oscar Cullmann, private conversation with author in Basel, Switzerland, 1986.

4. Jeanne Stevenson-Moessner, *The Spirit of Adoption: At Home in God's Family* (Louisville: Westminster John Knox, 2003), 111–14.

5. Seward Hiltner, *Pastoral Counseling* (Nashville: Abingdon, 1949).

6. Ibid., 283ff.

7. Ibid., 231.

8. Karen Scheib, "Older Widows: Surviving, Thriving, and Reinventing One's Life," in *In Her Own Time: Women and Developmental Issues in Pastoral*

Care, ed. Jeanne Stevenson-Moessner (Minneapolis: Fortress Press, 2000), 251–65.

9. Ronald Richardson, *Creating a Healthier Church: Family Systems Theory, Leadership, and Congregational Life,* Creative Pastoral Care and Counseling Series (Minneapolis: Fortress Press, 1996).

10. Susan Zerbe Pavelka, unpublished manuscript, Foundations of Pastoral Care course, University of Dubuque Theological Seminary, 2002.

11. Kathy Bonn, unpublished manuscript, Foundations of Pastoral Care course, University of Dubuque Theological Seminary, 2004.

12. Brian Pavelka, unpublished manuscript, Foundations of Pastoral Care course, University of Dubuque Theological Seminary, 2002.

13. Glenn Wilson, unpublished manuscript, Foundations of Pastoral Care course, University of Dubuque Theological Seminary, 2002.

14. Wendell Williams, unpublished manuscript, Foundations of Pastoral Care course, University of Dubuque Theological Seminary, 2001.

Chapter 7. An Alphabet of Grace

1. Jeffrey R. Zurheide, *When Faith Is Tested: Pastoral Responses to Suffering and Tragic Death,* Creative Pastoral Care and Counseling Series (Minneapolis: Fortress Press, 1997), 19ff.

2. Ibid., 38.

3. Suzanne Wobig, unpublished manuscript.

4. Anonymous, unpublished manuscript.

5. Dina Donohue, "Trouble at the Inn," in *Guideposts Greetings* (Carmel, N.Y.: Guideposts, 2004), 3–5.